STAINLESS STEEL BUTTERFLY

STAINLESS STEEL BUTTERFLY

Building a Strong Foundation
SO YOU CAN FLY

SUSIE PINKARD

Foreword by *New York Times* Bestselling Author ANDY ANDREWS

Niche Pressworks
Indianapolis, IN

Published by Niche Pressworks; NichePressworks.com
Indianapolis, IN

ISBN: Paperback   978-1-962956-14-7
        Hardback   978-1-962956-13-0
        eBook   978-1-962956-12-3
        Audiobook   978-1-962956-15-4

Table of Contents

"If"

If you can keep your head when all about you
    Are losing theirs and blaming it on you;
If you can trust yourself when all men doubt you,
    But make allowance for their doubting too;
If you can wait and not be tired by waiting,
    Or, being lied about, don't deal in lies,
Or, being hated, don't give way to hating,
    And yet don't look too good, nor talk too wise;

If you can dream—and not make dreams your master;
    If you can think—and not make thoughts your aim;
If you can meet with triumph and disaster
    And treat those two impostors just the same;
If you can bear to hear the truth you've spoken
    Twisted by knaves to make a trap for fools,
Or watch the things you gave your life to broken,
    And stoop and build 'em up with worn-out tools;

If you can make one heap of all your winnings
    And risk it on one turn of pitch-and-toss,
And lose, and start again at your beginnings
    And never breathe a word about your loss;
If you can force your heart and nerve and sinew
    To serve your turn long after they are gone,
And so hold on when there is nothing in you
    Except the Will which says to them: "Hold on";

If you can talk with crowds and keep your virtue,
    Or walk with kings—nor lose the common touch;
If neither foes nor loving friends can hurt you;
    If all men count with you, but none too much;
If you can fill the unforgiving minute
    With sixty seconds' worth of distance run—
Yours is the Earth and everything that's in it,
    And—which is more—you'll be a Man, my son!

— RUDYARD KIPLING, 1865 –1936

Foreword

Deep thinkers make thinking deeply look easy. It is not. It is, however, a process available to mere mortals like you and me. And no secret code is required to enter this incredibly valuable portal of understanding.

By their explanations, deep thinkers alert us to a spark of possibility that seemingly didn't exist a moment before. It is a flicker of promise transferred by a commonsense conjurer of bread to those who are perpetually hungry.

Deep thinkers explain the world around us in a way that not only makes sense of the complicated but becomes usable. To someone like me, the process has always appeared miraculous.

In my almost two-decade-long friendship with Susie Pinkard, I have become increasingly interested in the depth of thinking she has developed, for it has long shown evidence of a fortune in wisdom to be mined by anyone in her presence.

For a long time, those with access to her wisdom only included her family, friends, and a vast network of business folk who knew there was a difference-maker in this woman. Now, a great deal of that wisdom is available to anyone who reads — and thinks deeply about — the contents of this book.

From the starting point of a teenage "moment" in which her stepfather began reciting an old poem, Susie has lived her life taking steps that have been wisely chosen and understood.

In *Stainless Steel Butterfly* — a memoir that is at times equally funny, tender, and heart-achingly close to home — Susie delivers the very real story of "her life so far" in a way that can change readers' lives from now on.

Each chapter begins with a separate line from Rudyard Kipling's classic poem, "If." From those starting points, the author shares her journey in the context of what Kipling described as a wholly successful life.

He wrote those four eight-line stanzas of advice to his son in 1896. Although not published until 1910, the poem has inspired the world for a century. In these pages, however, Susie goes well beyond mere inspiration. By having "thought deeply" throughout the years about these words and their practical meaning, she has delivered a masterpiece that I dare say will be part of the conversation whenever Kipling's verse is delivered from this day forward.

This work is appropriate for young people, teachers, the newly married, those who are searching, pastors in need of sermon material that connects with ordinary people, and those who have never entered a church in their lives.

In closing, I can only urge you to read this book with a highlighter as if searching for answers that will change your life. And if you have the courage to think deeply about what you have highlighted, your life will indeed be changed.

— **ANDY ANDREWS**
New York Times bestselling author of *The Traveler's Gift* and *The Noticer*, CEO of CreatingMeasurableResults.com

A Stainless Steel Butterfly

Teenagers are rarely free of drama, and my teenage years were no exception. On this particular evening, I was standing in the kitchen, hair still full of saltwater, and my bare feet dusting the floor with a fine coating of sand.

I waved my arms, tears of frustration threatening to spill out of my eyes as I gave my mother and stepfather a blow-by-blow account of the latest soap opera episode with my group of friends. Probably about some boy. And probably more dramatic than it needed to be.

My mother, as always, moved about her work as she listened empathetically, adding a comment every so often to let me know she was paying attention.

As the youngest of seven kids, I was a natural peacemaker. I hated any kind of conflict. "The day started out so great," I complained. "Why can't they just get along? Why do they have to make such a big deal about everything? And why does it bother me so much?"

As a young girl, it was common that I'd get pulled into the emotions around me. I'd start out as positive and happy but would soon be sucked into the tidal wave of conflict around me. That's what was happening that night with my friends. "I just want everyone to be happy, and *I* want to be happy," I cried, throwing a look at the plaque that had hung in our kitchen for as long as I could remember. It contained a quote from Ralph Waldo Emerson and read, "Be happy, for every minute you are unhappy, you lose sixty seconds of happiness."

My stepfather, Ray, had been sitting quietly, listening to my tale. Suddenly, he spoke up and said in a firm voice, *"If you can keep your head when all about you are losing theirs and blaming it on you ..."*

I turned to him. "What did you say?"

Instead of answering me directly, he kept going:

> *"If you can trust yourself when all men doubt you,*
> *but make allowance for their doubting too ...*
> *If you can wait and not be tired by waiting,*
> *Or being lied about, don't deal in lies ...*
> *Or being hated, don't give way to hating,*
> *And yet don't look too good, nor talk too wise ..."*

My confusion turned to clarity. He was quoting a poem, something he did fairly often. This one sounded familiar, but I couldn't recognize it right away.

He continued: *"If you can dream — and not make dreams your master; if you can think — and not make thoughts your aim ..."*

He recited the whole poem in a voice that commanded attention and made it clear that what he was saying was important. And then, I recognized the poem as one of his favorites, "If," by Rudyard Kipling.

"... If you can talk with crowds and keep your virtue,
Or walk with Kings — nor lose the common touch,
If neither foes nor loving friends can hurt you,
If all men count with you, but none too much;
If you can fill the unforgiving minute
With sixty seconds' worth of distance run,
Yours is the Earth and everything that's in it,
And — which is more — you'll be a Man, my son!"

"Susie, I want you to learn this poem, memorize it, and live your life by it," Ray told me.

Being a teenager, I responded predictably. I rolled my eyes and said in a sassy voice, "I'm a *girl*. I won't be a *man*."

"You," he answered, looking me in the eyes, "will be a stainless steel butterfly."

> Stainless Steel gets its "claim to fame" due to its ability to resist rust and corrosion. This property is due to the addition of chromium, which creates a chromium-oxide film on the surface when exposed to oxygen. This film acts as a barrier between the steel and the environment. If the film is broken, it has the ability to self-heal, as long as oxygen is present.[1]

That was not the answer I was expecting. But like the poem, the words carried weight, even if I didn't fully understand them at the moment.

I don't remember the rest of that conversation over four decades ago, but I do remember that it made an impact.

---

1 "The Importance of Stainless Steel," Multiteria, 15 Nov. 2021, www.multi-teriausa.com/blog/the-importance-of-stainless-steel/.

The conversation — and the poem — was something I'd return to again and again in the upcoming months and years. It became a touchpoint for Ray and me, something we'd throw back and forth as I memorized it, quoting lines to each other. Eventually, it burned into my subconscious, becoming part of me and my psyche.

I've turned to different parts of the poem at different times in my life. While, at first, the lines would come to me as an afterthought, over time, they became something that was ready and waiting when I was struggling at work or in my personal life.

When I was faced with a set of circumstances I wasn't sure how to handle and wished I had on-the-spot guidance from a mentor, the poem would run through my mind, and somehow, almost magically, I'd land on just the right stanza at just the right time. It wasn't long before my thoughts shifted from "What in the heck do I do?" to "What in the poem might help me in this situation?"

Slowly but surely, my mindset about the challenges I was facing was changing. And when I shared these stories with Ray, he'd say with a smile, "There you go, being a stainless steel butterfly."

Over time, how I behaved was changing, too. Instead of reacting immediately, getting carried away with the emotions of the moment — both mine and others — I could take a deep breath and choose my response. I was becoming less influenced by the people and occurrences around me, and I could act intentionally. It became a foundation that supported me in some of the toughest times in my life. I was becoming, as Ray predicted, a stainless steel butterfly. I was learning when to fly, when to bide my time, and when to seek shelter.

Rain doesn't harm butterflies. They live through storms. But they rarely fly in heavy rain. Instead, they land and wait for the rain to stop and for their bodies to dry before they fly again.[2]

This poem guided me through the summer after my final year of high school as I transitioned to college.

It guided me through college when I ended up in a school far from where I thought I'd be, having to forge a new identity for myself ...

It guided me through meeting and marrying my husband and creating a new family unit ...

It guided me through early motherhood when I was trying to figure out how to balance kids and career ...

It guided me through ups and downs in my career for a Fortune 50 insurance and financial services company as I moved across the country and back again ...

It guided me through my husband's cancer diagnosis and his subsequent death when my world was turned upside-down ...

And it continues to guide me today.

I consider myself blessed to have had many sources of wisdom and support in my life. I had my mother. I had Ray. I had my older brothers and sisters. I had this poem. I had numerous mentors and advocates throughout my life who held my hand, listened to my challenges, and provided wise counsel. They all helped me develop the confidence, strength, and roots to keep me grounded when the world around me was shifting.

---

2 "Weather and Releasing Butterflies." Butterfly Fun Facts, 24 Jan. 2018, butterfly-fun-facts.com/weather-and-releasing-butterflies/.

Unfortunately, that kind of support system is becoming all too rare.

Two-thirds of Americans report feeling lonely,[3] with young adults reporting the highest rates of loneliness.[4] Twenty percent of people say they have no one to talk to about important matters.[5]

These statistics are depressing on their own, and even worse when I see them in the faces of people around me. There are so many who need guidance. I have friends in the corporate world who are navigating office politics, leadership, and the challenges of a post-COVID world, often while trying to juggle demanding home lives. Through my work at my alma mater, Jacksonville State, I see young people who are confused and disappointed by the tumult and division they're emerging into, and they don't know where to turn for trusted guidance. Then, there are people like me who are emerging into the next chapter of their lives and unsure of what is next.

I see hopeful people who simply do not have the community around them to provide structure, support, and encouragement when the rest of the world begins to shake.

It's not surprising that we feel like we're living on a cultural fault line. In recent years, many of the structures we believed would support us have been negatively impacted by the discord that exists around us. Government,

---

3 DeAngelis, Tori, "Young Adults Are Still Lonely, but Rates of Loneliness Are Dropping Overall," Monitor on Psychology, American Psychological Association, 1 July 2023, www.apa.org/monitor/2023/07/young-adults-lonely-pandemic.

4 Elias, Mark, "49 Loneliness Statistics: How Many People Are Lonely?" Discovery ABA: At-Home & Center-Based ABA Therapy (No Wait List), Discovery ABA, 26 Feb. 2023, www.discoveryaba.com/statistics/loneliness.

5 Elias, "49 Loneliness Statistics: How Many People Are Lonely?".

education, health care, families, religious institutions, small businesses, and even massive corporations have all been shaken, leaving many not knowing where to turn for certainty and comfort.

Now, when tough times hit — and they will! — many don't know how to move forward with confidence and the belief that they can handle what life brings their way. They don't know what to trust, what to question, and where "north" is on the compass.

On the Alabama Gulf Coast, where I grew up and now spend much of my time, storms are nothing to play with. They may bring torrential rain, damaging winds, storm surge, and more. They can sweep in and completely devastate an area in a matter of minutes.

There's nothing scarier than being in the midst of one of life's storms and having nowhere to turn and no idea what to do next. After all, when the storm hits and the winds begin to howl, even butterflies will look for something to clutch onto or a place to seek shelter. And life can become very confusing when everything you relied on as permanent changes with no warning.

Instead of being stainless steel butterflies, riding out the gale with confidence and strength, you become thrown about and often damaged in your heart, soul, and mind. You are driven by external forces, with no say over your own path.

The problem isn't that you aren't capable or strong or smart. It's simply that you never learned how to ride out the storms or how to determine when — and where — to seek shelter.

We've become a society of lost souls, fearful and timid — the exact opposite of what is needed in this place and time. We need leaders; we need light-bearers; we need people of hope and purpose. But who will mentor and develop them? Who will pour time, energy, and love into them? Who will guide them? How will they become equipped to take on challenging situations with grace and virtue? That's what I think a stainless steel butterfly is: Someone who can deal with a specific set of circumstances with steadfastness, calm, and dignity because they have a guiding set of principles to call upon.

It's into this landscape I offer this book and the stories it contains. I've pulled anecdotes and events from my life to illustrate the power of Rudyard Kipling's wisdom and words. From barefoot summer afternoons crabbing with my cousins to being on a stage in front of hundreds of insurance professionals, I've mined my own life for experiences and the lives of others to show how the right word at the right time can make all the difference. When you can have grace under fire, it is one of the most freeing experiences you can have.

I hope this book — and Kipling's poem — will provide a foundation for your life, equipping you with the tools to create your own foundation that will see you through the hard times ahead.

The poem "If" was a gift to me at a crucial time in my life when I was searching for a truth to hold on to. It's in that same spirit that I now offer it to you with love.

— Susie

SUSIE PINKARD

CHAPTER 1

Keeping Your Head

If you can keep your head when all about you
Are losing theirs and blaming it on you . . .

If you grew up on the Alabama Gulf Coast before 1980, I can pretty much predict what your summer looked like. You probably spent more than one steamy hot day on the waters of one of the numerous bays that pepper the area, hoping to bag some blue crabs.

This was my summer schedule when I was eight or nine. Several days a week, I'd head over to visit my cousins who lived in Fort Morgan on the farthest west point of Mobile Point, a narrow peninsula of land that separates Mobile Bay from the Gulf of Mexico. At that time, the area was little more than bait shops and fishing holes, and my aunt would give us each a quarter and a ball of twine and send us on our way. That quarter was enough to get a pint of ice cream and some raw chicken to use as bait — and enough to keep us out of her hair for a few hours.

We'd head to the Fort Morgan pier, a long, wooden structure that extended into the bay, high above the lazily swirling blue-green waters. We'd tie a bit of raw chicken onto a length of twine and dangle it into the water far below. Then we'd hop from foot to foot, the sun-beaten boards of the pier hot and rough beneath our bare feet, as we waited impatiently for the tug that let us know we'd gotten lucky.

Once we felt that telltale pressure, we'd slowly pull the twine, hand over hand, hoping not to disturb our prize at the end of the line. If we pulled too fast, the crab might let go, dropping back into the water with a disappointing plop. But if we were diligent and didn't move too quickly, we'd be rewarded with a fist-sized crustacean that we could detach from the line and toss into an old bucket we had on hand to hold our prizes.

That first crab, so rudely separated from his watery home, will do his darndest to escape. He'll scrabble at the sides with his lopsided claws, trying to pull himself up and out so he can return to the warm waters of the sea. He'll be so desperate to get out that if you don't put a cover on top of the bucket, you can't be surprised when you return later, only to find the bucket empty. After all, who can blame him for trying to find a way to freedom?

But here's something that I have seen to be true …

If you put two or more crabs in that same bucket, you can forget about the cover because there's no way they'll get out. Why? Because as soon as one crab tries to get out, the other crabs will block his escape. They'll grab at him and pull him back into the depths of their prison in a sort of crabby mob justice, almost as if they're saying, "Hey, where do you think YOU are going? If we're going to be someone's supper, you're sticking right here with us." It doesn't matter that they are pulling one of their own down into danger. If they're stuck, everyone else needs to be stuck, too.

Something I've also seen to be true is that people, unfortunately, are often not much smarter than crabs.

In times of threat, when emotions run high, that same mob mentality takes over. Instead of working together or offering support, many people try to bring others down, blaming them for their own troubles. Instead of appreciating that someone is staying calm and plotting a path forward that could potentially save them all, there's often an internal urge to keep them from succeeding.

Whether it's someone else finding a way to turn a catastrophe into a victory, rising above challenging circumstances, or maintaining grace in the face of adversity, others take it as a personal insult. Maybe seeing men and women who keep their wits about them makes some people feel like they're being judged for not doing the same. Or maybe they think that if more crabs are in the same condition, their chances of ending up on someone's dinner table are smaller. Safety in numbers, misery loves company, and all the other sayings prove to be all too true.

Thankfully, we're not crabs. We're not in a bucket. We have a choice when we see this dynamic at work or in our personal lives. We can be like the crabs and wallow in our misery, insisting others stay at our own level. We can make a half-hearted attempt to escape the current predicament, only to be snapped right back into the bucket by the grasping claws of others. Or we can, as Kipling urges us, keep our heads when others are losing theirs.

We're all faced with scenarios like this all the time. One I recall all too clearly was in the early 2000s. I had recently been promoted to an executive leadership role in Florida as vice president, agency — a new position and a new territory for me. Florida was reeling from eight back-to-back hurricanes, and it had adversely affected the insurance industry. The state had been experiencing a surge in claims, leading to increased costs for insurance companies. Add governmental pressure to increase discounts and lower rates, and many insurance providers were withdrawing from the Florida market altogether while those remaining were facing insane pressure. Many agents were experiencing huge cuts in their incomes and were wondering how they would survive financially.

It was in this atmosphere I landed — literally. Our company was flying in a team of executives to hold a series of meetings with our agents throughout the state. The goal was to brief them and talk about solutions. We were focused on moving forward, but our agents had a different mindset. They were looking for the ones responsible for getting them out of this enormous mess, and their eyes were pointed right at my senior vice president, Joe, and any other leader who represented their market. Although I was brand new to the role, I felt an incredible sense of responsibility.

Joe stood up on the stage in front of 300 or so agents, answering questions to the best of his ability and keeping his composure. But as his time to depart came closer and closer, it was clear that the agents were not satisfied. They had more questions and wanted — demanded — answers.

Amid the onslaught of questions, Joe, beloved and known in the company as something of a wildcard, looked at his watch. "I'm sorry. I have a plane to catch to meet with another group of agents in the Panhandle. But I've got someone here who will take over the discussion. I want to bring your new VP of Agency up here."

With that, he motioned to me. I stood up and began to walk over to the side of the stage where I could walk up the stairs to join him — a safer option in my skirted suit and heels. Instead, though, he motioned for me to approach him where he stood at the front edge of the stage. He reached out his hand and, in one motion, pulled me very ungracefully onto the stage to stand beside him.

"I'm leaving you with your new VPA, Susie Pinkard. She'll take it from here." And with that, he hustled off the stage, leaving me in the firing line.

When Joe left, about a third of the audience followed him out, figuring I had nothing useful to add. I took a moment to size up the remaining 200 or so agents, none of whom looked particularly friendly at that moment. As I gathered my thoughts, another bunch of agents gathered in the back of the room, separating into several groups who began loudly talking among themselves.

I was tempted to jump off the stage and join them. I had NOT been expecting to be left here to speak for the company and offer a sense of stability to a group badly in need of it. So, I picked up where Joe had left off, calling on those who had questions and doing my best to respond appropriately.

Unfortunately, the groups in the back of the room were so loud that I couldn't hear the audience members, and they could barely hear me, even with a microphone. The anxious chatter of the people in the back of the room was drowning out anything I said.

Panic rose in my throat. What could I say or do that would make any difference when a third of the audience had walked out, a third wasn't listening, and the third that was still listening couldn't hear a word I said? It would have been easy to freeze or flee, but thankfully, another option came to mind ...

> *If you can keep your head when all about you*
> *Are losing theirs and blaming it on you ...*

I tried to imagine what it would look like to keep my head, even with so many others giving in to the emotion of the moment.

Could I stay grounded while everyone around me was looking for a scapegoat? Would it matter if I did?

As I looked at each person sitting, watching me, I realized what the overwhelming emotion in the room was — it was fear. I could see it in the eyes of the younger agents who had just started their businesses and were wondering if they'd made a terrible mistake. I could see it in the eyes of the older agents, who could see decades of effort in building a family business being threatened. And I could see it in the eyes of the agents who had been in business a decade or so, seeing their livelihood crumble before their very eyes.

I understood them. They were feeling abandoned, threatened, and scared. Many had seen their incomes decimated and had no idea when or if the market would recover. They weren't necessarily blaming me, but they were blaming the organization I represented. They didn't believe I had anything to offer them — and quite frankly, I didn't at that moment. While I understood the economics of the circumstances in the state, I had no specific recommendations for how we would recover. For that, I'd need the cooperation, input, and trust of those sitting in front of me. The big question was whether I could bring them together so we could escape this bucket together.

"What have I got to lose?" I asked myself. I took a deep breath, surveyed the crowd in front of me, and silently held my arm high above my head with a single finger raised.

In a moment or two, the groups in the back realized their conversations were no longer competing with my voice over the sound system, and they began to quiet down. Those in their seats were obviously wondering what in the heck I was doing. But soon, the room quieted enough for me to be heard. "I need your attention for just one minute," I said clearly, speaking to those in the back. "Those who are here up front want to talk about solutions to this problem. If you'd like to participate in that conversation, please come up here. You're welcome to have your own meeting, but I need to ask you to take it outside."

Faced with that choice, about a third of those in the back left, but two-thirds took their seats. When the meeting started again, I was able to set the tone for a more positive discussion. "I don't know exactly what you're going through, but I can imagine," I told them. "We don't have control over what's going to happen in the legislature or politically. But there are still things we can do. And I'd like us to use this opportunity to share ideas about how you can work through this in your business so others can learn."

The rest of that meeting wasn't entirely positive, but it changed the focus of the conversation. Instead of looking for someone to blame, the agents began sharing resources and brainstorming. That discourse touched on a lot of points that eventually became part of the broader solutions for addressing the challenges of the Florida market. In fact, that meeting became the basis of a strong, trusting relationship I built with my new territory. Years later, people would mention that to me as the first time they'd met me, and they were impressed with my calm and confidence. I had kept my head, and it had paid off.

When you're faced with attacks, disagreements, or other challenges, remember this lesson from the crabs. You do have a choice in how you respond. You can sink into the muck, or you can try to rise above it. If you decide to use your energy to bring others down or you allow others to knock your legs out from under you, the only thing that happens is that you all end up in the stockpot.

CHAPTER 2

Trusting Yourself

If you can trust yourself when all men doubt you,
But make allowance for their doubting too . . .

When I was a senior in high school, my future was mapped out. Like many of my friends, I was going to attend what was then Troy State, a four-year college just over three hours from my home on the Gulf. I was going to major in music and march in the band, and I had a small music scholarship and a boyfriend who would be waiting for me back home.

That is, until my college plans started to fall apart bit by bit. And then my parents dropped a bomb on me.

"You're going to Jacksonville State University in north Alabama."

Ummmm. *What?*

This was not what I had expected. I had it all planned out, and JSU — over five hours away — was *not* part of the plan.

And that was exactly what my stepfather, Ray, wanted. He wanted to shake me up, but good.

Before my father died and my mom met and married Ray, I lived a pretty small life. I am the youngest of seven stairstep children — three girls, three boys, and me — and we all lived in a 1,100-square-foot house. My parents were hard workers, but with seven young children, there was never enough money to go around. We had the basics, and my parents loved us and each other, but our perspective was limited to what we saw around us.

When my father passed away at age forty-five, things got even tighter. My mom worked long hours as a restaurant manager, money was even tighter, and that was just how life was.

When my mother met Ray, he loved all seven of us as his own. He was a successful real estate developer with no children of his own. He entered my life at age fifteen, and at that point, he introduced me to a world I didn't even know existed.

Ray saw how limited my life had been. He knew I lacked confidence and cared too much about what others thought. He wanted more for me, and he and my mother were willing to do what they needed to shake me up.

The first piece was getting me out of South Alabama, away from the familiar existence of being "Susie Smith," and into a new environment. That meant JSU.

If their goal was to shake me up, it worked.

I had expected to head off to a college that would allow me to be who I was in high school. I expected to join the band, major in music, and continue hanging out with many of the same people I'd spent the last four years with. But that all disappeared in a matter of minutes.

The scholarship, the friends, the band, and even the boyfriend were gone, and I had to find a way to replace them. Like the poem said, I would need to trust myself to find my way. That's exactly what Ray wanted for me.

Despite my insecurities, I was determined to make the best of the situation. If my mom and Ray thought I could succeed at JSU, they must be right.

Since I enrolled in JSU so late in the summer, I couldn't join the band as they'd already been on campus practicing for days by the time I arrived. I longed for some sort of structure and connection to fill the hole my friends and music had once occupied. Somehow, I heard about a JSU institution — the JSU Marching Ballerinas, a dance team that performed with the band. If I made the team, I wouldn't be playing music, but at least I'd be on the field with them.

To my surprise (since I'd never had a dance lesson in my life), I made the team and found a new group of friends. On campus, I also joined a sorority, declared myself a finance major, and soon found my place at my new home. My stepfather Ray had been right. I wasn't lacking like I thought I was, and my old life didn't define me. I found a new sense of confidence where before there'd been insecurity. I had learned to trust myself.

It's hard to learn to trust and believe in yourself, even when you have a strong cheering section like I had with my family. It's even harder when those around you doubt your abilities and aren't shy about sharing their skepticism.

Early in my career, I encountered many people who judged me at first sight, and often, my looks worked against me because I'm about 180 degrees from your stereotypical corporate executive. Female, short, blond, and Southern — I'm no stranger to people writing me off when they first meet me before I even open my mouth. I'd gotten used to that, but I wasn't prepared for someone doubting me after I felt I'd spent years paying my dues and proving myself over and over again.

I was very blessed in my time with my company. I was promoted numerous times, and no one had ever expressed doubt in my leadership capabilities. In fact, I was often picked for leadership roles and put in positions before I thought I was 100 percent ready.

When the next promotion came, and I wasn't certain I was ready, I'd tell myself, "I guess I can do this — after all, they chose me." I never found myself having to prove anyone wrong about their belief in me; my goal was always to prove them right for trusting in me and giving me an opportunity.

That's why it was such a shock when that moment of doubt came. It was in my early months in a new role in Florida as a vice president, agency. My husband Chuck had just been diagnosed with brain cancer, and life was swirling around us. With two teenagers, an ill husband, and no idea what the next years would bring, it seemed wise to try to relocate to be among our friends and family in Georgia as we navigated Chuck's illness.

I asked my boss at the time, Bill, if he would approach the senior vice president, Jim, and ask him if he would support my request for a lateral move to return to Georgia if a position should become available. Jim's response was puzzling. It raised the question of whether I should take a role with less responsibility, given the extreme business and personal circumstances.

I was confused. Chuck and I had sacrificed so much to achieve the position I was currently in. We'd moved around the country willingly, uprooting our family again and again. I had no idea what was in front of me, but I didn't want to simply walk away from what we had achieved. That meant meeting with Jim face-to-face — to understand how he viewed me and my capabilities.

With Bill's blessing, I had the opportunity to meet with Jim before an executive meeting. I told him, "Jim, Bill and I have talked about your response to my request, and I want you to know I am as committed now to my role as I would be otherwise."

It was kind of an absurd thing to be saying. The company was facing a market crisis in Florida and financial threats. I was still new to the role, and I had a terminally ill husband and two kids. And I'm sitting there, calm as can be, having coffee with a senior vice president and assuring him I'm 100 percent committed and none of that was going to affect my job.

Jim just looked at me, then said, "Susie, I appreciate what you're saying. But this is going to affect your job. There's no way this can't affect your job."

That's when I got mad. I think I hid it well, but I was seething. Suddenly, I had to prove Jim wrong. But I knew showing him my anger wouldn't convince him of anything. Then, Kipling's words in this stanza made complete sense: I had to make allowance for his doubting.

I gathered my composure and looked back at him. "Jim, under the circumstances, I can understand why you believe what you believe about me. I'm new to this market. We've got a crisis. And I've got a terminally ill husband.

So, I can totally see from your perspective why you don't think I can do this job without my performance being affected. But let me make you this promise. I am going to be as cognitive as I can be about my performance, and I want honest feedback about how I'm being evaluated." He nodded, and I continued.

"One thing you can be assured of is I'm not going to take advantage of this organization. I have very high standards for my performance, so if I find myself in a position where I'm not able to meet those standards, I will know it before you see it. And I promise you'll be the first one I'll inform if I need to call myself out."

I could tell he was thinking over what I'd said as he excused himself to take a phone call. But as I left, I said to him, "Don't be surprised at what you might see." The confidence Ray knew I'd need in my later years had grown and bloomed.

I wasn't sure if I'd made any impact, but I'd done what I could and had to leave it at that.

Later that day, as I was driving home from the executive meeting, Bill called me and said, "I don't know what you said to Jim, but the level of respect he has for you has elevated beyond anything I could have anticipated." I told Bill, "All I told him was that I'm going to do my job to the best of my ability and be very conscious of my performance. I want feedback, and I want to know if I'm not being perceived as performing at the level you expect, regardless of the circumstances. And I told him I'll be the first to raise my hand and step down if I can't meet expectations because I care that much about this organization."

Now, I didn't talk to Jim in order to debate his concerns. I said what I did because I believed wholeheartedly in my ability to meet the company's standards and also in my willingness to step down if that's what was best. I wanted him to know that I trusted myself even in the midst of understandable doubt. I had committed to him that I would do the job, and if I couldn't, I'd step aside.

Months passed, and I simply did my job and cared for my family, doing what I had to do. And then, six months later, when we were preparing for another surgery for Chuck, I got a call from Bill. "There's an opening in the Georgia market," he said. "It's being offered to you as a lateral transfer. Do you want it?" My answer was immediate: YES. We were being offered the gift of being able to return to Chuck's home state where we could be surrounded by family as we faced this next chapter — all because I'd not only trusted myself but made room for others' doubting.

A few days after Chuck passed away, I received a random phone call. "Hi Susie, it's Jim. When you are retired like me, you sometimes receive word a little late. I just heard about Chuck's passing, and I wanted to tell you how sorry I am for your loss. I know it was difficult, but you put Chuck and your family first while handling the demands of your role. You should feel good about that." That call meant a lot to me.

CHAPTER 3

Letting It Play Out

If you can wait and not be tired by waiting . . .

If you've ever seen a newly mature butterfly emerging from its cocoon, the process is probably not what you expected. It is not a grand unveiling of a breathtaking creature emerging from its cocoon in one split second, unfurling its multicolored wings in a grand show. Instead, it is tediously slow, taking anywhere from a few hours to a day or more. The butterfly struggles against its confines, fighting to break free, its wings folded tightly to its body.

Watching this spectacle, you might be tempted to assist the poor creature. It's working so hard, and all it would take is a slight bit of effort on your part to make its journey to freedom so much easier.

But if you were to try to help by opening the cocoon, you'd actually be destroying the butterfly's chances of survival. The struggle and the time taken for emergence are essential for the butterfly's physical development. The struggle is part of the essential path to maturity. Without it, the butterfly's wings would never gain the strength needed to fly. By removing the struggle, you've removed the resistance needed to support it on its future flights.

As hard as it may be, we must step back and remain spectators. Behind those tiny, fluttering wings is a story of strength, transformation, and a fight for survival that turns a caterpillar into the majestic butterfly it's meant to be. We need to have patience as nature takes its course.

Patience. We all know we need it, but it is something that does not come naturally to most of us. Especially for those of us who strive to be high performers, we want to jump in and solve problems. When those problems impact those we care about, the desire to fix them gets even stronger. As a mom, it has been especially hard to back off and not fix every challenge my kids face.

This is not an endearing parenting quality. Just as with the butterfly, it might seem great in the short term, but in the long run, we're actually hampering our kids — and our employees and team members — if we constantly fix things for them. That's because they don't learn to act on their own. They don't learn to trust themselves. They don't develop the skills they need to navigate their way in the world. They don't earn their strength and confidence. Instead, they learn only to rely on us.

I was such a great fixer with my kids. When they were younger, that might have meant talking to a friend's parent to resolve some issue the two children were experiencing or providing resources to solve a situation. My daughter, Suanne, in particular, has always known that she can come to me, and if I have any capacity to make things better or easier, I will. She's even had times as a teenager when she'd be in some adolescent crisis, and she'd come to me and cry, "Fix it, Mom!" I would go into a tailspin until I could find a way to fix whatever was wrong.

I know, not good. I did too much. I was not allowing my children to handle their own challenges and have their own consequences to learn from. I was helping them out of the cocoon rather than watching them struggle on their own so they'd be better able to handle life in the future. I needed to have patience, to wait it out, to be an observer of the struggle.

Here's the good news: I'm getting better. I am learning to be more of a coach than a fixer. Because my daughter is now running a business in the industry where I spent over three decades, she often comes to me for advice on how to handle specific challenges. But telling a grown adult how to fix their life is very different than calling another parent to discuss how to help our children get over hurt feelings so they can all be friends again.

These days, I can tell Suanne exactly what I'd do to handle an employee or policy issue, but that's not going to help her grow into her leadership role. And even when I do give her "the answer," more often than not, it doesn't go well. In one recent conversation, I said, "Suanne, I can't help you. Nothing I'm telling you is working." She answered, "Mom, that's because you're not telling me the right thing! What is the right thing?" Believe it or not, it's actually good. It means she's struggling to figure it out. She's strengthening her wings. She is learning to fly.

Now, I try to take more of a coaching approach with her and anyone who comes to me for guidance. It's harder in some ways because I often feel like I could fix the problem pretty easily, but I realize I must be patient. I have to back off. I have to wait as they find their own way.

Even when I believe I could fix things for others with the "right answer," it might not be the right answer *for them*, as I learned with Suanne. I don't want to be responsible for the outcomes of someone else's life. I don't want to assume things or make decisions that might go against their values and principles. I don't want to make a call that could negatively impact someone personally or professionally when I don't have all the details or when our values differ. That's why waiting and patience are such huge lessons to learn.

Someone who emphasized the importance of timing to me was the agency vice president I reported to when I had my assignment in Florida, Bill Roundtree. He was the master of knowing when it was time to act and when it was time to have patience and let things play out. As you might imagine, this was a tough distinction to grasp for an action-oriented person.

Before moving onto Bill's team as his direct report, I'd been in a role in Bloomington, Illinois, at the corporate office that was all results-based. My job was to keep things moving forward and to do so with as little delay as possible. Suddenly, when working with Bill, I might identify a problem and present a solution to him, only to have him tell me, "No, not on this one. This one you need to let play out." At first, I didn't understand. If there was an issue and I determined how to fix that issue, why wait? Wasn't the goal to fix the problem as quickly as possible?

Not always, as I learned from Bill. If I didn't know all the information or if the situation would shift over time, then the best course of action was to wait. If I acted immediately, I might only be solving part of the problem, and the problem could get bigger. In fact, by acting too soon, I might actually contribute to the problem getting bigger. Some problems, Bill taught me, aren't ready to be solved when we are ready to solve them. We simply want to get them off our plates and move on to the next thing. If I adopted a posture of watchful waiting, though, the problem would sometimes resolve itself, or the answer would reveal itself. Additionally, that answer might be a much better approach than if I'd tried to act too soon.

The longer I could stay in the question, even though it was uncomfortable, the more complete my understanding of the problem would be.

Bill learned this lesson through his own challenges. A dedicated athlete, he was the leading high school basketball scorer in Missouri state history, breaking the record of Bill Bradley, an Olympic gold medalist who went on to play for the New York Knicks. He expected his career would continue in college.

But when he got to the University of Missouri, he didn't get much playing time during his first year. He chalked it up to joining an experienced team and looked forward to seeing more action when he returned as a sophomore. Unfortunately, he still wasn't playing a lot, and while things started well in his junior year, he soon found himself on the bench. "I came really close to leaving, but something told me this is where I needed to be," he said. "My four-year career was a great experience, but it wasn't what I thought coming in. So I talked to my college basketball coach, and he said, 'Son, sometimes during the course of life, you just have to let it play out.'" Bill remembered that advice and took it to heart. Now, he looks at his time at Mizzou as one of the best decisions of his life because it put him in contact with people who would impact his career for decades to come.

"Sometimes things are right in front of you, and you just want to attack it. You want to make this decision. But sometimes you have to take a step back and say, 'Is this one of those situations where I just need to let it go?' That has driven a lot of decisions in my life," he explains.

And because Bill shared this perspective with me, it's also driving my life.

When learning this lesson, I had to fight my natural tendencies. I was afraid that I was actually contributing to a poor outcome by not doing anything. I had to ask myself, "If I don't do anything about this right now, what will happen? How severe is it going to be? Who's going to be impacted by it and to what degree? If I don't take care of this, who will?"

In some cases, I might realize that if I didn't do anything immediately, the problem would not get any worse. In fact, if I didn't do anything tomorrow, things would be pretty much the same. But if I put off acting for a week or more and it could become a bigger issue, that's a clear sign a decision needs to be made.

The key is to let your decisions be driven by need, not simply because you have grown tired of waiting.

CHAPTER 4

Truth, Love, and Humility

Or being lied about, don't deal in lies,
Or being hated, don't give way to hating,
And yet don't look too good, nor talk too wise . . .

Sometimes, the truth hurts. We often avoid the truth because it is painful to give and painful to receive. We want to be nice, so we avoid tough conversations, and we avoid giving — and receiving — the honesty that can help us grow as people.

The key is giving feedback with love and humility and receiving honest feedback without letting our ego or our hurt feelings blind us to the seed of truth that lies in criticism. Particularly when in leadership positions, our team's trust in us must be paramount. They must know we have their best interests at heart and that we will treat them with scrupulous integrity. We need to know them as people, not just as a means to achieve a corporate end. If we don't approach them as people with complete lives outside the workplace, we'll fail miserably. And that's exactly what happened to me back in 2011.

I had just returned to a vice president role in Georgia, and the team I was working with was underperforming. My goal was to get results and to get them fast. There was one gentleman, a field executive named Troy, whose performance was not at an acceptable level. We'd been working together for several months, and his territory was continuing to underperform. I set up a phone conference to go over all the issues one by one. These types of conversations are never fun, but I could sense that Troy was not at all receptive to me as I pointed out the gaps in his territory and all the ways he and his team needed to improve.

Finally, he said, "Do you know what I did before I joined this company?"

I said, "Well, I've seen a jersey hanging in your office. I think you were a professional football player."

Troy said, "Yes, I was. Do you know what team I played for?" I had to say no.

Then he asked, "Do you know my wife's name?" I was taken aback, but I shook my head and said, "No, I don't."

"What about my kids' names? Or the sports they play, do you know them?" Again, I had to say no. He went on this way, asking me four or five questions about him and his personal life. And I couldn't answer a single one.

I was appalled at myself. I'd always prided myself on knowing my team members and how to tap into what motivated them. Here was a key team member, and I was failing miserably. He wasn't the only one underperforming. I had let him down. That truth was hard to swallow, but I could not deny it.

In previous positions, I had really taken the time to get to know my people, learn how to lead them, and understand the market circumstances. I had not done so in Georgia. I was familiar with the market and my role, and I even knew many of the people in the area, so I thought I didn't need to do the groundwork I had done in the past. And that was a huge mistake. Here was someone who wanted to be known, but I hadn't taken the time to initiate the conversation.

I sat silently for a moment and then said, "Troy, I want to start over with you. I want to reset. I want to know you and your family." So we dropped the conversation about performance and instead focused on him. I learned about his wife and his kids. I learned what sports they played and what activities they participated in. And I learned that when Troy was in high school, a coach basically told him that he would never succeed. That coach's lack of belief in him fueled Troy to put in the work to prove his coach wrong. He became an excellent football player, earned a college scholarship, and was drafted by the New England Patriots.

When I finished talking to him, I was almost in tears. I knew I had failed as a leader by not getting to know and understand the people I was leading. I had been so focused on the business, so focused on a result, that I failed on an important principle that I had exercised many, many times before in many, many roles: Get to know your people. This principle was fundamental to who I was as a person and as a leader, and Troy called me out on it.

Thankfully, Troy was willing to forgive me and re-start our relationship. He told me, "I want you to take a little sticky note, and I want you to put today's date on it. Put it in your drawer because on this date next year, we're going to be looking at my performance, and you're going to be telling me how proud you are of me and what I have accomplished."

Troy wasn't making excuses for his performance. He simply pointed out, "If you want me to perform, this is what I need from you as a leader. I need you to know how I'm doing. How's my family doing? How are my children doing? I want to be able to share with you their successes and what is important to me."

And guess what? A year later, we weren't just applaud-ing him for the improvement; we were applauding him for being at the top of my entire team. He was proudly walk-ing across the stage and getting awards at different events, shaking the senior vice president's hand. And it started not with him but with me.

I had no excuse for overlooking this principle. I'd known it for a long time, but in my focus to get results, I'd forgotten.

Fortunately, Troy reminded me. Because of my interac-tion with him, I recommitted to leading people first, not results first.

A person who comes to mind when I think about leading with humility and love is Angela Martin. Angela was one of the leadership executive development associ-ates who reported to me when I oversaw the Executive Development program. My role was to work with these individuals, coach them, and track them along with their assigned work. I monitored how they were learning, what they were learning, how they were growing, and how they were performing, all in a very strategic and intentional manner. The goal was to prepare them to assume a vice president position.

Angela was very easy to connect with from our very first conversation. She had a level of mental maturity and a calm disposition that demonstrated her humble confidence and strong sense of self. One of the things I appreciated most about her was her consistency; she was the same person personally and professionally with an open heart and a genuine interest in others. She had a lot on her plate with both a young grandchild and older children in her home. But I know that whether Angela was walking into her home or the office, the fundamental qualities of who she was as a human being were always there. Empathy, compassion, trust, accountability — she not only led from that place; she lived from that place.

Seeing people as part of the work team and as individuals was a critical element of her leadership style. Over time, I had the opportunity to see her handle numerous challenges with grace. Whether it was serving as a peer leader to other people in the development program or dealing with the terminal illness and subsequent death of her father, Angela was a perfect example of personal and leadership strength.

She was a living, breathing example of the power of empathy as she showed commitment to her team as they managed the challenges of their roles and the challenges of life. Many leaders don't care about the personal side as long as the team achieves the desired results. But Angela always understood that employees are people first. Unfortunately, this is what I missed with Troy. I was only looking at the numbers, not at the man, and he knew it. He told me plainly that if I expected him to give his all, I needed to respect him and get to know him as a person.

Influential, compassionate leaders don't start the discussion in job performance conversations around performance — or lack thereof. Instead, they start the discussion around the individual performer. They recognize the need to lead the person as a whole, not just as an employee — not just the salesperson, not just the stock boy, not just the server at a restaurant ... as a person first and foremost.

Of course, there are limits. Caring about a team member is not an excuse for a lack of performance. I'm not saying it's the leader's responsibility to take on that person's personal problems or even to help them resolve them. It's not the leader's responsibility to make accommodations for that person's poor performance. But a caring leader will be interested in what's going on with that person and at least open up the opportunity for that person to share what they feel comfortable sharing.

This is where Angela shone. She knew intuitively that someone's personal issues don't get put in a box from nine to five every day. Instead, what's happening in that person's home life could be getting in the way of them performing at their best. Listening to others honestly, compassionately, and with a humble heart matters. You just may be the one who makes a significant positive impact by being able to say the right thing at just the right time. But if we don't practice these basic human qualities as a matter of daily principle, we will often miss opportunities right in front of our eyes.

This people-first principle is missing in a lot of businesses. We're so focused on numbers, metrics, or goals that we look at our team members like they are just employees existing to serve the organization. We're missing the opportunity to treat our employees as whole people. Sometimes, they do not need someone to give them a pass on their performance. They do not need you to own or resolve their issues. More often, they need a simple acknowledgement of what they may be dealing with. When they know you care, they know they can trust you. They can trust you to have their back, to give them necessary feedback in a constructive manner, and to have open conversations. That type of trust gets built by being as interested in the person as you are in the performance.

Building that kind of relationship takes time, but it's worth having those casual exchanges about weekend plans and family vacations that may seem unimportant. It's worth following up and asking about a child's college plans or cheerleading camp. Each of those conversations is a brick in the foundation of trust. And it's that foundation that makes the difference between a good leader and a great leader.

That carries over into all relationships, personal and professional. It goes for parenting, friendships, and marriages. When you focus on the person, when you focus on the positives, they'll give more. They'll feel noticed and appreciated. They'll feel valued, and they'll value you in return.

CHAPTER 5

Dreams

If you can dream — and not make dreams your master ...

If you call someone a dreamer, it's a bit of a backhanded compliment. While it's wonderful to have goals and ambitions, if you live too far in the future instead of embracing reality, you can spend a lot of time and energy focusing on what is *not* rather than what *is*. Dreams are great, but being so absorbed by them that you are dissatisfied with your present doesn't serve anyone, particularly yourself.

It's a balancing act. How do you design a future or choose goals that excite you and pull you forward without becoming completely unhappy with your current situation? That's something I had to learn the hard way.

Chuck and I were college sweethearts, and we got married in 1985, shortly before I graduated. We moved to his hometown of Rockmart, Georgia. At that point in my life, I was still immature in many ways. Other than going to college, I'd never been away from home or my family. I'd never traveled anywhere.

While I was so excited to be married and I was completely in love with my new husband, I was also struggling. I had been taken from a world I knew and plopped into a completely different environment. Rockmart is a small town in northwestern Georgia, and Chuck's family were fixtures in the community. We had a lovely little home just steps away from his parents, and we were beginning to make great friends. I had all the reasons in the world to be happy, but I wasn't.

I was homesick — for my family, for the beach, for Alabama. I didn't know how to make this nearly constant feeling of sadness go away.

Thankfully, I met Deborah Helms. A chance conversation with her helped me reshape my perspective at that point in time and for decades to come.

Deborah's husband, Bobby, had been friends with Chuck for years. Deborah and Bobby had been married a few years longer than Chuck and I, and they had a toddler son named Clint. Bobby and Chuck were both on the town council, and Deborah and I became fast friends. We'd often travel together to conferences, and Deborah and I would hang out with Clint at the pool while the men attended their meetings.

The thing that immediately struck me about Deborah was her attitude. Here I was, with everything in the world to be happy about, and I always had this rain cloud over me. No matter how wonderful things were, I was finding fault with everything around me. It wasn't that my life was so hard and full of problems; it was my mindset that was out of whack.

One day, I was in the middle of yet another conversation about how sad I was and how homesick I was when Deborah said something that was like a light going on in my head. She said, "I just believe happiness is a state of mind. It's a choice."

Wow. For whatever reason, Deborah's words struck me so deeply right then. All of a sudden, I realized I had a choice to be happy. I could miss my hometown. I could miss my mother. I could miss my stepfather. And I could still choose to be happy with where I was. I could dream about being closer to my home, but I could choose not to let those dreams rule me.

Thankfully, I know wisdom when I hear it. I was able to take that "Aha" moment and turn it over in my brain, seeing the truth in it. After that, I committed to not having a negative, unhappy view of life. Thanks to Deborah, I was in control and now realized it. She showed me what life could look like if I could just manage to shift my thoughts.

What I remember most about Deborah is that she was always upbeat, always smiling, always laughing, saying something funny, and showing interest in other people. She motivates others just by being around them. I admired her, so why wouldn't I take her advice?

As I was writing this book and thinking about her huge impact on my life, I felt called to reach out to her directly to find out how she has maintained such a positive mindset for as long as I've known her.

Her story makes me even more impressed with the way she's lived her life. It wasn't that she has been spared struggle or pain. Instead, she just chose to greet each day, choosing to be happy.

Deborah says she's always been an optimist, even though she wasn't brought up that way. When she met her mother-in-law, Alma Helms, Deborah was impressed with how funny, kind, and loving she was. At one point early in her marriage to Bobby, the couple was struggling with infertility, a challenge that could easily lead to depression. Around this time, Alma and Deborah were talking, and Alma mentioned her belief about happiness being a state of mind. Just as Deborah's words struck me, Alma's words struck Deborah. She resolved that she would stay positive whether or not she ever got pregnant. She would dream of becoming a mother, but she wouldn't allow that dream to steal her joy in the present.

Thankfully, Deborah and Bobby went on to have Clint, but even if they had not been blessed with a child, I believe she would have kept her positive perspective.

As human beings, our natural state is to be unsatisfied. We're built to push ourselves. Especially for those who are driven, it's natural to have dreams and long for things we don't currently have. But if we center our happiness on something or someone else, we'll always be dissatisfied and disappointed.

For me, "dreaming, but not making dreams your master" means you cannot put off your life or your happiness until you achieve everything you want — whether it's a car, a person, a job, a house, or a certain goal weight. You'll never get there when you place your happiness outside yourself and your current circumstances. Even if you achieve your goal, happiness will continue to be just out of your reach. It will be a new job, a new car, or a different weight. The pursuit just never ends.

But if you start with the mindset of choosing happiness, you can stay in the moment. You can have a wonderful life at the same time you're pursuing your dreams. You can add things and people to what you already have, but you don't need them to be satisfied.

After this conversation with Deborah, things shifted for me. I didn't immediately stop missing my family. I still missed them, but I started looking for — and finding — opportunities around me. From career opportunities to connections, there were tangible things I could appreciate in my day-to-day life. Before Deborah's wise words, I thought about happiness as something that happened to me. If something good occurred, it was a good day. If something bad happened, it was a bad day. It was up and down, up and down, depending on what happened *to* me. But once I believed I was in control and had a choice, I could start behaving and thinking that way.

This mindset became a habit for me over the ensuing years. I worked hard at training my mind to look for the gifts in the present instead of constantly being focused on the future or on what I didn't have. Over time, it became easier and easier, and that practice came in handy when there were situations where things were far from ideal. After all, problems, big and small, are part of life. No one is spared from challenges, and I'm no exception. One time in particular gave me the perfect opportunity to put my chosen optimism to the test.

My career required many moves for our family, some being tougher than others. We made our first move as a family to Cumming, Georgia. There were a lot of positives about that move, but it was still difficult for all of us. We are small-town people at heart, and we'd moved into a very nice golf club community in a larger city. The community was gorgeous. There was a lake in the middle with a fountain, and mallard ducks roamed the streets. We lived in a wonderful neighborhood with great schools, but something was still not sitting right with me.

Work was getting stressful, and I had this low level of anxiety that would bubble up on occasion. I remember driving home from work one day, and it all settled on me. Worry and a bit of depression were creeping over me as I realized the big responsibility that was resting on me — to work with an underperforming team. I was trying to figure out a strategy for getting that accomplished, and so for the drive home, I was focusing on all that was hard in my life. But then, as I got to the gate of our community and saw the lake, fountain, and ducks, I remember thinking, "Why am I letting myself go down this path? This is my choice. I have every reason to be happy."

It wasn't a huge moment, but it was significant. It was one time when I clearly remember choosing to think differently based on my self-talk. I shifted my thoughts, and I did so purposefully. After all, you won't always have your best friend sitting beside you to remind you. You have to be your own best friend. That was the lesson I learned from Deborah.

I want to be really clear about something. I'm not saying that I recommend people ignore their emotions. Sadness is part of life. It's okay to be sad because certain things break our hearts. But we can't stay in sadness. At some point, we have to move on. We have to find a way to break out of the mindset that is holding us back from the joy that we need in our lives and that God intended for us.

This became abundantly clear to me as my family faced many ups and downs through the years, including challenges in work, personal life, and Chuck's illness. I had already been practicing not letting future dreams be my master. During these tough times, I continued to focus and train myself to embrace the moments I had, and to choose to find pockets of happiness where I could.

It's fine and good to have dreams, but you cannot be so absorbed by and fixated on those dreams that you ignore what's right in front of you. No matter how big our future is, we need to live in the present and enjoy what we have, being grateful and appreciative. Gratitude grounds us in the here and now. When you practice gratitude, you automatically become happier because you focus on what you have, not what is lacking. Some of the happiest people in the world have very little, but they recognize and are grateful for what they have.

I also think some of the most grateful people are those who have lost much. They know how quickly things can shift. So much can change in just one day. You'll never regret learning to love the life you have right now.

CHAPTER 6

Thoughts and Actions

If you can think — and not make thoughts your aim ...

I have met many great thinkers in my time, but I will be the first to say that while great thinking is admirable, it's not enough. To make a difference in life, you have to take action.

We all know people who talk a good game. They do all the research. They plan and review and plan some more, but their plans never turn into anything because they do not take action. Procrastination has killed more careers, dreams, and potential than just about anything else. Put it this way: even the most risky venture has a chance of succeeding, however slim it might be. But if you never try, your chances of success are zero.

I've hired many people over the years, and one of the qualities I've always considered the most important was a candidate's ability to take action. Particularly in sales, people need to be action-oriented. As every salesperson knows, sales is a numbers game. You make a certain number of calls, which yields a certain number of appointments and generates a certain number of sales. Make more calls, and you make more sales. Decrease your activity, and your sales drop as well.

Of course, a lot more is involved in the sales cycle, but the relationship between activity and outcome is pretty clear. There are very few ways around this reality, and that became clear to me when I was working with an employee I'll call Robert.

Robert was one of my direct reports. He wanted to move into an agent position, which requires a great deal of sales expertise. To develop his skill set, I put him in a position where he could learn the fundamentals of the agency business model by working directly with agents. It was an opportunity to observe firsthand everything involved in successfully launching an agency. The idea was that he'd build his knowledge and experience and eventually become an independent business owner, running his own agency. From training to prepping to product knowledge to developing a strong business plan, he'd be ready with all the pieces in place before launching.

Robert was a conscientious, diligent employee. During the first phase, he was very successful, and I was completely confident in my decision to move him into an agent role. I had observed his thought processes, and I saw that he clearly understood the overall business. I also thought he was action-oriented since he'd done a great job of meeting and even exceeding expectations and goals in his current role.

When Robert launched his agency, he had a solid business plan in place. He was taking over the role of a retired agent, so he had a book of business and a nice, solid group of clients to work with. He even had a seasoned team member who would join him, providing continuity for the clients and insight into the market. Essentially, the only things that would change were the name on the sign over the door and the person sitting in the agent's chair. It really was an ideal situation for a new agent to launch successfully.

It wasn't long before I saw some cracks. Within the first month, I noticed that Robert's production wasn't what I expected, especially given all the tools and benefits the office already had when he started this agency. I went through the normal process of coaching and looking at what, in my experience, was typically the issue: the sales process. But the process Robert had in place was solid. To make sure, I went through some role plays with him, where I played the client, and he'd walk me through the various products. Clearly, Robert had great communication skills and knew how to understand the client's needs and present products to match.

I was puzzled. Robert had all the pieces in place, so what was the issue? Maybe it was just a temporary lag, so I decided to give him another month to see if things improved. They didn't. He explained that he just couldn't get the clients in the door, and without appointments, sales would naturally be affected. My next suggestion was to look at his marketing strategy. We identified a few places where we could make some adjustments, and he agreed to give it a go. We both felt confident that production would pick up.

The next month, though, things were no better. Here we had a very smart man with solid processes and an experienced team. The office environment seemed positive. Robert was, in all respects, a fairly good leader. So what was the issue? At this point, I asked myself, "What have I *not* examined? What am I *not* seeing?" And the answer was so basic that it was no surprise I had overlooked it: his calendar.

Robert had the knowledge, skill set, and leadership ability, but there was nothing on his calendar. He had no activity. He wasn't making calls, which meant he wasn't booking appointments, which meant he wasn't making sales. It was really that simple.

Even after working with him in a very focused manner, he was unable, on his own, to make the calls needed to generate the production needed to keep his office afloat. When I dove into why he couldn't make those calls, I realized that it was simply not in his skill set. When I asked him, "Robert, are you coming into this office and doing what you need to do every day?" And he answered, "No. I can't make myself do it. I can't do it."

He wasn't a lazy man. I had seen him be very successful in a different role. He just could not act without someone else standing over him, telling him what he needed to do. He couldn't stand hearing "No." He couldn't even stand the possibility of hearing "No." And so he avoided the task altogether. He could think through things, but he couldn't act.

At that point, we had to have some honest conversations about Robert's future as the head of his own agency. If we moved forward, he simply would not be able to manage on his own. Because of his inability to take the needed action, it was clear to us that it was not the right fit for him. Thankfully, we were able to transition Robert into a role that was more in line with his strengths.

Some brilliant people are strategists who can come up with all the plans in the world. They can think creatively and insightfully, but their gift is not execution. They need to either partner with someone who can execute on their behalf or find a way to move beyond the procrastination that keeps them stuck in their thoughts.

Procrastination can hit any of us at any time. We are all susceptible, and just because we are action-takers in one area doesn't mean we won't get stuck in another area.

I have always been an action-taker, especially at work. That's why I was caught a bit off guard when I found myself having trouble moving forward.

After Chuck died, I wasn't motivated in the least on a personal level. I was motivated from a business standpoint because business was my escape, my outlet. But I had no motivation to do anything else. I didn't want to change one single thing. I wanted it all to stay just as it was. Chuck's Bible and his glasses were still in the exact place where he had left them. His shoes and socks were still inside his closet in the exact place where he had left them. That would be understandable if it had only been a month or two, but it was a full eighteen months, and I was unable to move forward. Like Robert, I couldn't make myself take action. I couldn't take the steps to move forward.

For a while, living like this was a comfort for me because it gave me a way to continue to be in Chuck's presence even though he physically wasn't there. I would even crawl into the bed we'd brought into the house during his illness just to be in his presence. For a while, I thought it was healthy. But after eighteen months, I couldn't justify it anymore. I realized that by remaining in this state of inaction and not taking steps forward left me stuck in a world that didn't exist anymore. I was trying to hold onto something that was already gone, and I knew something needed to change.

So, I took what I thought was a small step. I picked up the phone and called a friend who is a real estate agent. I told her I was thinking about moving. "I'm just considering it," I told her. That small opening was all I needed to break the dam that had been holding me back. "Let's just put up a 'for sale' sign and see what happens," my friend told me.

There's a saying that when you take a step forward, the universe will rise to meet you. In this case, I feel God's divine action met me. In a matter of days, I got an offer on the house with the provision that I needed to be out in three weeks.

The dam had broken. I was moving forward whether I felt ready or not, and I was doing it quickly. It's no surprise that this was a jolt to me, but having to make that move in a matter of weeks — having to go through my possessions to get rid of anything I wasn't going to keep, having to find temporary housing — it was what I needed to do to move forward in my life. I think God knew that, left to my own devices, I'd stay right where I was for the foreseeable future. A big shakeup was the only way to get me out of my rut.

What finally motivated me to pick up the phone and make that call was the realization that my inaction wasn't just impacting me. It was affecting my kids, too. My refusal to move forward was keeping them stuck as well. Any parent will tell you that we'll do things for our kids that we're incapable of doing for ourselves. Letting go of that house helped me move on in other ways, too. I started to embrace my new life as a single woman rather than as part of a couple. Life wasn't turning out to be what I thought it would be, but it was still good in many ways, and I was glad to be able to move into this new stage.

I think we sometimes don't take action because we don't want to move on from where we are, either because we fear the future or don't want to let go of the past. But staying in our thoughts — whether rooted in the future or the past — isn't the solution.

Thoughts are, of course, important. They are the foundation of ideas, plans, and beliefs. They shape our perspective and guide our understanding of the world. However, thoughts on their own are dead. It is action that brings those thoughts to life and creates tangible results. Without actions, thoughts remain as mere potential.

We can sit around and think about things all day long. But if those thoughts do not lead us to anything meaningful, we're wasting our one precious life.

CHAPTER 7

The Balance Between Triumph and Disaster

If you can meet with Triumph and Disaster
And treat those two impostors just the same . . .

Chuck and I met during my sophomore year at Jacksonville State University. We were set up by my sorority sisters, who assured me we'd get along great. A year older than I was, Chuck played on the college golf team, had blond hair and blue eyes, and everyone agreed he was just the nicest guy. They were right.

It wasn't long until we started dating seriously and spending more time together. I knew things were getting even more serious when Chuck invited me to watch him play in a golf tournament. I had never been golfing, attended a golf tournament, or even watched golf on TV, so this was a big deal.

"I tee off at 8:05," he said. "Whatever you do, don't be late!"

Of course, I was late. I think I was just getting in my car for the long drive at 8:05, and I rolled up to the golf course that was hosting the tournament closer to 9 a.m. Fortunately, I spotted JSU's golf coach, who recognized me and told me where to catch up with Chuck's foursome. "Just follow this path. You can't miss them," he told me.

I walked along the path, taking in the setting where Chuck spent so much time. It wasn't long, though, before I lost track of the path and found myself on the edge of a clearing. I could see people ahead, so I wandered across the beautifully manicured grass, walking quickly to catch up.

Suddenly, I heard people shouting. I looked around but didn't see anything. More shouting, then I could see people waving — at me! Finally, someone came running up and said, "You're in the middle of the fairway! You need to move, or you're going to get hit!" Later, I learned the meaning of "fore," an important term if you're going to be walking in the middle of the fairway.

Whoops. I was obviously embarrassed at my ignorance, but I was still excited to see Chuck play. I finally caught up and followed along for several holes, taking in all the action. At one hole, it was clear he'd made a good putt as everyone was clapping. I was so excited I ran across a sand area to give him a big congratulatory hug! Little did I realize that I'd just traipsed across a carefully raked sand trap. Chuck gave me a look that could freeze ice. By this time, I had made plenty of golf etiquette mistakes, and it was starting to unnerve Chuck. "You can't do that," he hissed, turning away to find a rake to fix the messy footprints I'd left.

I don't remember a lot more about that day other than that I was mortified by my missteps, and I would not have been surprised if Chuck never called me again.

Despite my lack of golfing etiquette, we continued to date and eventually became engaged. And now, when I think back on this day and my moments of despair, I laugh at that naive young girl who had no idea how many thousands of hours she'd spend on golf courses over the next three decades.

Isn't it funny how, over time, despair can turn into something lighter as your perspective shifts? That disaster of a day didn't stay that way. Chuck didn't dump me. He saw past my mistakes and looked at me — my character, personality, and strengths, not just my lack of golf knowledge. He knew that the mistakes I made that day weren't the sum total of who I was as a person. It was just one day in what would become a very long relationship. And while it seemed awful at the time, it is, in retrospect, a love story — our love story.

Of course, time has a way of flattening out the highest of highs and the lowest of lows. As I've experienced more of both over the course of my life, I've learned that there isn't always a harsh division between what is good and what is bad — what is a triumph and what is a disaster — because usually, everything that happens to us contains a little bit of both. Absolute black and white are rare; the sooner we can appreciate the shadows and gray areas, the more stable our life becomes.

And when the storms of life hit, we can all use more stability. When we feel like we're being hit from all sides, having a firm foundation under our feet can make all the difference.

When Chuck became ill in 2009, we were in the prime of our lives. He was just shy of forty-eight. We had recently moved to Florida from Illinois for my work, and I'd been appointed to a new vice president position. Chuck was so excited to be in a climate where he could golf more consistently, and of course, we all loved being closer to family in Georgia and Alabama. We had only been in town a few months, and we were just starting to make friends and get settled in our new neighborhood. By then, our son Charlie was out on his own, and Suanne was in high school. We found a picture-perfect home on the 17th tee in a golf course community, and I wanted to make our home special for my daughter and Chuck because they'd done so much to support me as I moved up the ranks at work. We were excited about this next stage of our lives.

One day in late May, Chuck came home from the driving range where he'd been practicing for the upcoming Florida State Amateur Golf tournament, complaining of a severe headache. Thinking he was just dehydrated from a long day in the sun, he drank water and tried to relax. The headache got progressively worse over the course of the evening, getting to the point where it was clear that something was very wrong. Even though he insisted he was alright, I got him in the car and took him to the emergency room. What we didn't know at the time was that his brain was swelling.

That night, even before the CT scan and the neurosurgeon and all the doctors and tests that would follow in the weeks and months to come, even before I heard the words "brain cancer," I knew that things would never be the same again for our family. Something had shifted, and I could feel it in my very core.

My immediate response was to go into research mode. It's almost like the emotional side of me shut off so I could deal with the crisis in front of me. The emotions were so overwhelming that I had to take myself out of the chaos. My children were devastated. Chuck's parents — who immediately left their home in Georgia to drive overnight to Florida — were devastated. And I needed to be the go-to person to stay in control.

That became my job — on top of my jobs as wife, mother, and executive. We would support Chuck through this process in every way possible: spiritually, mentally, intellectually, and emotionally. Our commitment to him, his survival, and his quality of life was absolute. He would have us as his team, no matter how hard things got.

And things got very, very hard.

Brain cancer is, within the world of cancers, very rare — only two percent. Chances are that even if you know someone whose life has been touched by it, you haven't heard the real story unless you are very close to them because nobody wants to share the ugly truth of brain cancer. It's bad enough to see your person diagnosed with a terminal illness and then have to see them go through the treatment process. But when you factor in the behavioral and cognitive changes, it's truly devastating. Surgeries and almost daily radiation for months on end, years of chemotherapy — all that ravages the body while the cancer ravages the mind.

Chuck had always lived an extremely healthy lifestyle. After college, he had considered joining the pro golfing tour, but he gave up that goal to raise a family instead. In his 40s, he was a better-than-scratch golfer and thought he might eventually retire early and play on the Senior PGA Golf Tour. When he wasn't golfing, he was working out. He ate well, was physically strong, and was very active. As an attorney, his mind was as vibrant as his body. He was full of life and full of dreams.

All that changed in a moment, and life changed for the rest of us, too. There were so many unknowns we were trying to deal with around Chuck. At the same time, my kids were growing into young adulthood, and I was struggling to find footing in my new work role. Every day brought more questions when all we wanted were answers.

As time progressed and a treatment plan became more clear, our lives developed a new rhythm, of sorts, with Chuck and his illness at the center. Every decision we made, individually and as a family, focused on the goal of giving Chuck everything he needed in every way possible. Our son Charlie moved to Florida to be closer, and in time, we relocated back to Georgia to be closer to our extended families.

Even with the best care, every day seemed to bring a new heartbreak as we loved Chuck through the ups and downs of an illness that would span almost seven years.

So much happened during those years. I lost count of the trips to the doctor, the lost sleep, the prayers, the tears, and the ups and downs. We moved and then moved again. We redecorated the house, we advocated, all in the pursuit of making Chuck as comfortable as possible. And over and over again, we consciously decided as a family that we were going to love him through this, providing him the best care and support emotionally, physically, and in every other way. That was going to be how we helped him. We would keep him for as long as God was willing to let us keep him.

Eventually, the cancer progressed, and surgery was no longer an option. Chuck was deteriorating very quickly, and we had to have that final conversation with his doctor, whom we had really grown to love. Everyone in the room — his parents, my daughter, my son, even the doctor — was in tears. And when Chuck eventually passed away, our hearts were broken.

Chuck's illness and death impacted so many people. I, of course, lost a spouse and best friend. My children lost their father. My in-laws lost a son. Chuck's sister lost a brother, and numerous people lost a friend. It is a wound that will never fully heal, and we continue to process our loss.

Even with all this, I cannot think of this time in our lives as a disaster. While I would never choose this path, I also refuse to ignore the gifts it brought us. So many people walked alongside us in very real ways. We found humor even in the darkest times, choosing to laugh when we easily could have cried. We pulled together as a family to surround Chuck with all the love and support we could, giving all we had, even when we thought we had nothing left to give. We all deepened our faith as we faced challenges we could never have handled on our own. We grew to appreciate each additional day we were given with Chuck, knowing that none of it — the good or the bad — would last forever.

One of my greatest lessons from this time was the acceptance of the wholeness of life. Nothing is a pure disaster or a complete triumph. Both triumphs and disasters are imposters, hiding a richness beneath the surface if you are willing to look deeper. The peak experiences, the times of pure joy, are few and far between. If we wait for them before we embrace the life we have, we are overlooking moments of joy sprinkled all around us.

As I look at this next chapter of my life, it's not what I expected or what Chuck and I had planned so many years ago when we were newly married. But I believe my life is still good. It's still beautiful.

CHAPTER 8

Building Back

Or watch the things you gave your life to, broken,
And stoop and build 'em up with worn-out tools ...

Chuck gave so much of his life to golf. Even now, years after his passing and several moves later, I have a collection of his numerous golf clubs in my basement — not to mention dozens of golf shirts, tournament memorabilia, and more. After his diagnosis, Chuck lost many things, including his ability to practice law. But what was even harder for him was losing golf, which had been such a huge part of himself for almost his whole life.

After Chuck's initial diagnosis, surgeries, and treatments, we were given an incredible period of grace. His initial prognosis had been one to three years, and here we were at three years with things starting to stabilize a bit. He was still on chemotherapy and getting regular scans, but the disease was not progressing. We started to believe that maybe we could breathe a little bit and relax into this new normal.

At that time, Chuck was doing well spiritually and mentally. But physically, he was very weak and, of course, had not been near a golf club in years.

Around this time, I was introduced by my senior vice president to an amazing woman named Ouida Brown, who was a personal trainer and life coach. Through a series of conversations, I came to believe she could be just the person to help both Chuck and me regain some of the health we'd lost — Chuck because of his illness and me because I'd basically set everything aside to care for my family and do my job. I believed that if God was going to give us this time, we would be good stewards of it and do our part to bring ourselves to the best level of health possible.

In one of the initial conversations with Chuck, Ouida asked, "Chuck, what do you want to do? What are your goals for where you are in life right now?" That might sound like a strange thing to ask someone with a terminal illness. But Ouida didn't see Chuck as a patient or someone who was broken; she saw him as a man with a future ahead of him. That was a gift.

Chuck answered, "There are two things I want to do. I want to practice law again, but I know I can't do that. I don't have the memory or the deductive reasoning because of the amount of brain tissue I've lost and because of where the tumor still is, so I know that's not practical. The second thing I want to do is play golf. I believe I can do that again. I want to be able to play and play in tournaments. I want to be able to play for fun and get back to the best of my capabilities, whatever that is."

Ouida listened and then simply answered, "I think we can do that."

Those words, that belief in him, gave Chuck so much hope. He had something to look forward to, a future that went beyond his illness. It didn't matter that he felt like he was starting over from scratch. What mattered was that he had a goal he was excited about.

Ouida and Chuck began plotting out his return. He knew he had to get his strength back. With the approval of Chuck's doctor, Ouida put together a plan, and they began to work on everything from his strength to his mobility. It was intense. Sometimes, after their sessions, he'd just sit in his chair, absolutely drained. Finally, one day, he said, "If I'm going to work this hard, I'm going to do it on the golf course."

Even that was a big stretch. One of the side effects of his tumor and the surgeries was that he'd lost his equilibrium, and just swinging a golf club was too much. In fact, when Chuck swung his club for the first time, he nearly hit the ground because it made him so dizzy. But little by little, he started making progress.

For Christmas that year, we set up a room in our basement as an indoor practice spot for him. We carpeted the room in astroturf and installed a big net to hit into. We hung inspirational art on the walls, alongside all of his trophies and plaques from tournament winnings, to give him even more motivation. We named it the "We Love Chuck" space. We wanted to give him a place where he could start to get back to what he'd loved so much but that he'd lost over the previous few years.

After a few months, he was ready to go out to the golf course. He wasn't able to play a whole round at first, but just playing outside was such an achievement. The muscle memory started to come back as his body remembered what it felt like to swing a driver, to putt. He was progressing in inches, not in miles, but each new milestone was worth celebrating. It felt like he was coming back to himself.

This period was a gift. He joined the Northwest Georgia Senior Golf Association and played in tournaments — and he was winning! Chuck never returned to the plus-two-handicap golfer he'd been before his illness, but for the next two years, he was able to play. And he kept improving. He even qualified to play in the Georgia Pro-Am tournament. Unfortunately, he was only able to complete the first two days of the four-day tournament because walking eighteen holes a day was beyond his endurance. But instead of being frustrated and angry, he was so excited and proud. He was able to look back at where he'd been and see how far he'd come. He'd been so weak, and his body had gone through so much. But he'd set a goal to golf again, and he had more than achieved it. He focused on that rather than on what he'd lost.

I think that's the time when he came to terms with what he would be capable of. He knew that, at some point, he would not be able to play anymore. Of course, he hated that knowledge, but he was able to look at what he'd done and have gratitude for what he'd overcome.

There are comeback stories where miracles occur, and the cancer goes into remission or the tumor disappears. I wish that was our story, but it's not. The cancer did progress, and eventually, Chuck did have to give up golf. Seeing him navigate this process, though, was such an example to me and to the kids. Here was someone who had every reason to give up but instead said, "I'm going to do what I love to the extent possible for as long as possible." And then he made it happen. Chuck showed us all that everything can be taken from you, and if you have the determination, you can refuse to stay beaten.

We face this same challenge to different degrees throughout our lives. Businesses fail, relationships break down, storms come, buildings are leveled, and everything we invested in can be taken from us in an instant — something we know all too well on the Gulf Coast. When that happens, we have a choice. We can sit in the wreckage of what was, or we can grab our shovels and our hammers and start building again, board by board.

Personally, I've lost people I've loved. I've lost positions I've loved because of reorganizations. I've built teams to success and then been asked to leave and do the same for a different team in a different city or a different state. And honestly, it was sometimes hard to look at what was in front of me and say, "Here I am again, starting over." But every time I did, I learned so much in the process.

A few years after Chuck died, I was asked to relocate to our company's headquarters in Illinois. The position was a promotion, and while I was honored to be asked, it was a decision I wanted to carefully consider.

Moving to the company headquarters was intense in many ways. Being literally under the nose of the highest executives in the organization brought with it a level of scrutiny. And because many of the residents of the town also worked for the same company, it felt like you were always on display. You couldn't go anywhere — a restaurant, the mall, or a grocery store — without running into people who knew you or at least knew of you. You really had to be on your best behavior at all times.

Chuck, the kids, and I had moved to the headquarters in Illinois as a family many years before. But now, I was being asked to return as a single woman, starting from scratch at a very different place in my life.

I knew if I did accept the role, I wanted to do things differently. I didn't want to live in a neighborhood full of families where I would feel out of place. I also knew that if I were to make the move, I wanted to create a new home on my own terms — something just for me and for where and who I was now.

This time, I wasn't looking for a neighborhood community because I didn't have a family with me. I wasn't going to be active in a school environment because I didn't have a child in school. And I wasn't going back with a spouse that I could socialize with.

Instead of buying a house, I wanted something different. I visited an upscale apartment in a more urban area, close to restaurants and boutiques and near a university. The second I saw it, I knew it was where I wanted to be. It was all brand new and very modern, with a really cool lobby. I decided right then that this would probably be the one and only place that I would ever live that would be 100 percent about me. I'd be living by myself, I wouldn't be entertaining people here, and I wouldn't need to accommodate other family members. This was my one time to just be all-out girly. For the first time in my life, I selected the furnishings and decorations aiming to please only myself, not three other people. I bought a pink sofa, a deep shag rug, and interesting art. I embraced all the feminine elements I wanted. I told myself that this would be my escape, a place no one else but I needed to appreciate. And so "Susie's She Shed" was born.

During this time, many weekends, I'd travel by myself to Chicago, a few hours away. I'd spend the time walking the city, discovering new cafes and restaurants, and even going to live music performances on my own. It was all about exploration and new experiences, building a different kind of life. It wasn't always comfortable. Sometimes, I was lonely, and sometimes, I couldn't help but think about what I'd lost and how hard it was to be starting over again.

This time also brought gifts, though. I was learning to make decisions based only on what I wanted, not for my kids or for my husband. I was learning who I was on my own. The surprising thing was that when I embraced my new identity, others saw what I was doing and were drawn to what I was building. Even though I'd created a "She Shed" full of female touches, my son Charlie ended up feeling so comfortable in my new home that he moved in with me for a bit. I took visitors along with me on some of my Chicago adventures, and they loved the new restaurants and entertainment spots I'd discovered.

By becoming dedicated to what I wanted and needed and not worrying about anyone else, I created something others were attracted to. I was building a life that was just for me, and as I stepped into it, they fell in love with what it meant. I think they could sense my devotion to life in this different stage.

Getting a new sofa and exploring Chicago didn't make my grief evaporate. I still missed Chuck — and always will.

There are pieces of my heart that will never forget the life we had together because it was a good life. At the same time, I'm committed to building back. Will it be better than before? No, but it can still be good.

CHAPTER 9

Twisted Truths

*If you can bear to hear the truth you've spoken
Twisted by knaves to make a trap for fools . . .*

From the start, my brothers, sisters, and I all knew something was not right with the relationship between my mother and a new man she'd met.

My stepfather, Ray, had passed away about six months earlier. We were all heartbroken. He had been a constant presence in our lives for almost twenty years and had become a father figure for all of us. He had managed to do the impossible — win over seven individuals, fiercely protective of our mother, and establish a unique connection with each one of us. We were missing him, we were worried about our mother, and we knew something was wrong with this guy, Bob. The pieces just didn't add up.

I first heard about Bob when I called my mom at work one day. She owned a restaurant and was typically there fifteen-plus hours a day. If I wanted to talk to her, I had to catch her at the restaurant. This time, though, she wasn't there. "She's out with a friend," my sister told me.

Then, when I came home from Georgia for a visit, Bob was at my mom's house and was there the whole time I was home. I thought it was a little early to be getting seriously involved with someone else, but I knew how lonely she was. It wasn't long, though, before he sold his own house and moved in with my mother.

Bob was a charmer. He was an attractive man for his age, and he knew something about everything and had an answer for every question. Very quickly, though, we all started noticing discrepancies in his story. He said he was a retired biology teacher, but then when my sister, a teacher herself, tried to talk with him, it turned out he'd been a substitute teacher. There were no specific out-and-out lies, just gut feelings from all of us that raised some red flags.

That feeling was confirmed when I was visiting a year or so later, and my mother told me in a moment with just the two of us, "I've gotten myself into a mess, and I don't know how to get out of it." She didn't elaborate, and I didn't press. I waited for her to reveal more, but she never did. I regret not pushing, but it wasn't the nature of our relationship, so I just let that lie there, knowing she meant Bob but figuring that she'd tell me more when she was ready.

Not long after that, my mother was diagnosed with stage IV colon cancer. She went on to live seven more years, with Bob in her house the whole time. She had always insisted that she would never marry again, and I truly believe that from the day he moved in, he was laying the groundwork for a plan. We wouldn't discover the extent of his scheme for years.

At one point during her illness, at a time she was sure Bob was nowhere around, she showed me her will and her power of attorney document, with me named as her executor. "I know you'll handle this properly," she told me.

"What does Bob have to say about this?" I asked. She assured me that he had no say in any of it and was not included in her will. In fact, she told my sister, Janie, that upon her death, Bob was to vacate the house immediately.

It seemed to me then, and even more so now, that Bob had some hold over my mother. Maybe it was financial, or maybe he had some knowledge she did not want shared. She seemed almost scared of him at times. And what was amazing to all of us was that my mother was a very smart woman, yet she'd still fallen victim to a trap she couldn't seem to get free from.

As my mother's condition worsened, Bob tried to insert himself into decisions about her care. I had to step in multiple times with the doctors to show that I had her power of attorney and was her healthcare proxy, so I was the one legally appointed to make decisions on my mother's behalf. It got to the point that when my mother went into hospice, Bob was having side conversations with other relatives and the hospice nurse, trying to convince them that I had my own agenda and wasn't acting in my mother's best interest. In fact, he even introduced himself to the nurse as my mother's husband. I knew if I didn't correct him right there on the spot, that he would take that silence as agreement.

So I looked at him, and I said, "You are not her husband." Then I looked at the nurse, and I said, "He is not her husband. He has been her significant other for many years, and he has lived here, so he will be here. But he is not her husband." I thought that was the end of it, but the trouble was really just beginning.

Mama died thirteen days later, and my brother-in-law and Chuck sat Bob down and told him he needed to make plans to vacate the house. It was only a matter of days before his plan came to light. Bob went to a lawyer and convinced him that he was my mother's common-law husband and had every right to her estate, and we're all just a bunch of greedy kids trying to kick him to the curb. It soon became clear this wasn't a new thought; he had been trying to set this scenario up for years.

The standard for a common-law marriage requires that both people publicly recognize their relationship as one of marriage. Bob had laid the groundwork carefully. Every time he had visited the doctor prior to my mother's death, he listed her as his next of kin and her relationship as "wife." Thankfully, though, my mother had never referred to him as her husband. If she did include him on medical paperwork, he was listed as a "friend."

We were able to prove to the court that my mother did not consider him her husband, but it took fifteen months and a jury trial before we were free of Bob and his deception. Despite his lying on the stand about their relationship, we'd escaped his twisting of the truth.

The upside, though, was that our family grew closer during this time. With stress like the loss of a parent, compounded with a legal battle, it would have been easy for us to turn on each other — especially in a family as big as ours. That didn't happen, though. We treated each other with respect and care, and that saw us through. In retrospect, though, I wish I'd pressed my mother when she admitted to me she was stuck in his trap and wasn't sure how to escape. Even if we had known more about the situation, I'm not sure how we could have helped her, but we all certainly would have tried.

This story is a prime example of someone else laying a trap and attempting to ensnare us by twisting reality. Fortunately, I haven't run into a situation like this too often in my life. What I have run into way too often, though, is when I am the one who's trying to twist things around to suit my desires. Whether it's lying to myself or just refusing to hear anything contradictory to what I want to have happen, I'll admit that I can be my own worst enemy, working against my own good. Talk about being a fool! There is no bigger fool than one who won't be truthful with him- or herself and instead twists the facts to make things turn out the way they want.

As a woman of faith, I challenge myself to seek God's counsel on difficult or complicated situations before I make a decision. When I do so, I find a lot of peace. It's not always that I hear a clear answer — though, at times, I do. Instead, I practice laying aside my desires and telling God that I want to obey his will, not mine. I make it his decision, and in letting go of holding 100 percent of the responsibility, I can have peace with whatever happens.

One time in particular, though, I clearly did not follow my own advice. I basically tried to outmaneuver myself — to make the decision and then turn everything inside out to make it the right decision.

At a certain point in your career at my company, you had to decide whether you'd be willing to relocate to the corporate headquarters if you were to be asked. If you chose not to go, you were basically telling the upper management that you were not interested in advancing, and you'd be pretty much removed from further consideration. As a result, you had to be pretty sure of what you wanted to do before the opportunity even arose.

My superiors had told me that I had been flagged as a "high potential" individual and, at any time, I might be asked if I was interested in advancement. "They're going to ask you, Susie. It's a matter of time. And when it's your time, you need to have made that decision," they said.

Now, I was not at all sure about what I wanted to — or should — do. I wasn't clear if I wanted to move into such a visible role. I wasn't sure I wanted to relocate my family again, and I was not sure I was ready for the move. At the time, my mother had just been diagnosed with colon cancer, and I used that as a legitimate reason to be put on hold for the next few months.

Soon, though, my mother's situation stabilized, and I could no longer use it as an excuse. I was told I needed to make a decision one way or the other, and if I chose not to move forward, my spot would be given to someone else. I had numerous talks with Chuck, asking him what he thought I should do. I wanted him to take the decision from me, but he just kept pushing back, saying, "If they ask you, you can decide then." He didn't fully grasp the fact that if they asked me and I said no, I was basically removing myself from further advancement.

Well, the opportunity did come, and I did say yes, but my heart was not at ease about it. I had not sought wisdom or counsel from God. Instead, I was trying to figure out what was right on my own, and then I tried to make it work. But everything about the decision felt wrong to me.

Our son Charlie was a senior in high school. I did not want to take him out of school, so I was commuting between Illinois and Georgia on a weekly basis, leaving my family behind and living at a Country Inn & Suites. I would fly home every Thursday night, work from home on Friday, and then return to Illinois every Sunday evening. I would show up in the office on Monday morning, pasting a smile on my face and trying desperately not to show how depressed I was without my family. It was torture.

Now, in the long run, everything turned out okay. Over time, I let up on the pressure I was putting on myself. Charlie graduated in June, and the family moved up to join me in Illinois. We settled in and began to make a new home together. But it was so very hard — harder than it needed to be, simply because I talked myself into a decision that I wasn't ready to make.

At that point in time, I should have asked to be left off the list. Instead, I gave in to the pressure that I was going to miss my chance; I was going to get passed over; I was going to get left behind. I didn't make the decision logically. I made it out of emotion. I let my fears overcome my better judgment, and I paid a price for that. Pretty quickly, I recognized that I'd forced the timing on something I should have left to God. I had set a trap for myself and fallen right into it.

What a valuable lesson on how easy it is to fool yourself! I learned by going through something like that and having to suffer the consequences of my own selfish decision-making, though. And I can use it as an opportunity to become wiser in the future.

CHAPTER 10

Risk and Loss

If you can make one heap of all your winnings
And risk it on one turn of pitch-and-toss,
And lose, and start again at your beginnings
And never breathe a word about your loss . . .

Some people seem to handle risk better than others. We've all met those folks who seem completely comfortable jumping into situations that the rest of us would see as completely insane. Whether it's putting money into a risky business deal, trusting someone with your heart in a new relationship, or betting on an unproven idea, they don't know the meaning of "moderation." They go all in.

My stepfather, Ray Dempsey, was an all-in kind of guy.

Ray met my mom in 1978. I never spoke to him about how he made his decision to go all-in with a widow with seven children or what he thought about us and about becoming part of our family. It was just who he was. He loved her; she loved him, so what was there to think about? We seven kids were just more people to connect with and love. The way he managed to create a unique connection with each of the seven of us was remarkable. We weren't one big group, "the kids." We were individuals, and he related to us in individual ways.

We weren't the only people he embraced this way. Ray had a group of buddies in real estate and construction who he'd meet for breakfast every morning at a cafe called Hazel's Nook. One day, their favorite waitress wasn't there when they first sat down. It turns out she had had car trouble. Right then and there, Ray decided the group should pool their money to get her car fixed. By the time breakfast ended, they'd pledged enough money to not only fix her car but to buy her a new one, no strings attached.

That was Ray — if he saw a need and he could help, he did without hesitation and without asking for anything in return.

I think my brothers, sisters, and I sensed this about him. Ray wasn't being kind to us as a way to win over our mother. He wasn't manipulating us. He wasn't expecting anything from us. He was just loving us, pure and simple. As a result, we welcomed him into our lives.

Ray lived life and conducted business the same way. As a real estate developer, he was used to taking big risks. He was instrumental in the development of the City of Orange Beach on the Alabama Gulf Coast. Before Ray set his mind to it, its landscape looked nothing like the mile after mile of condos, multimillion-dollar beach homes, restaurants, and retail outlets you now see when you drive Highway 182 down the length of Perdido Key.

Ray saw something more in those undeveloped stretches of beach, lagoons, and wetlands. He had a vision. He knew that eventually, people would get priced out of nearby Gulf Shores as it continued to develop, and they would be looking for somewhere else to go, preferably nearby. There would be money to be made for those who could provide alternatives. He became determined to be the one to provide it first in the form of The Breakers, a beachfront condominium development in Orange Beach — the first of its kind in the area.

In hindsight, looking at what the city has become, it's easy to say that the development of Orange Beach was inevitable. But in the early 1980s, it was a big risk. The area had been damaged by Hurricane Frederic in 1979. Despite the challenges and the numerous naysayers, Ray was able to gather together the resources, partnerships, and people to create The Breakers, an eight-story building with 34 two-bedroom luxury condos. Now, The Breakers is dwarfed by newer developments like Turquoise Place, which stands three times as tall. At the time, though, the development was literally groundbreaking, and its success was far from guaranteed.

But it did succeed, and Ray made a lot of money for a lot of people in the process. The thing about real estate development, though, is that it has big ups and big downs. You can't control the weather, the real estate market, or the banks, so a lot of his projects succeeded, but some failed, too. The thing about Ray was that he could be worth a few million one year and owe a few million the next year, and he seemed to be equally content in both situations.

I think the ups and downs were a large part of the fun for him. He'd come up with what others considered a wild idea, and then he and his friends would see if they could make it work. Sometimes it did, and sometimes it didn't. But win or lose, he would move forward to the next project. "They liked the thrill of the ride," Ray's friend John Bowman recalls. "I don't think he looked at the end results. Money wasn't the goal. He didn't live his life that way." He just wanted to see if it was possible, asking if he could make his vision a reality. The process of working toward that goal was its own reward.

Like all of us, Ray had his own demons. Life wasn't always easy. He had financial hard times. He struggled with alcohol to the point that he knew if he started drinking, he wouldn't stop, so he stayed away from it, at least for the first few years after he met my mom. Once he started, he took it to the extreme. When alcohol began to interfere with his ability to execute his business visions, he knew it was time to get help. I have so much respect for him for getting help when he needed it. I also believe his own challenges made him more compassionate to others who needed a hand.

Regardless of external circumstances, Ray seemed to maintain a sense of equilibrium through the roller coaster ride of life. In retrospect, I think he had a rare ability to figure out what mattered deeply and what didn't. For instance, fashion.

Ray was known for his wardrobe of Hawaiian Aloha shirts that he'd pair with white pants — always white, no matter the season. Not only did it make it easy for him to get dressed, but he also said he preferred white because he was a messy guy. If he spilled cigarette ashes or coffee on his pants or got dirty messing around some construction site, he could just bleach his pants back to white again.

His car was another item that was not high on his list of priorities. He drove an old Mercedes everyone called "Old Blue." Even though it was a four-door sedan, he could barely fit one other person in it with him because the back seat was filled to the brim with empty cigarette packs, empty cans, old papers, and food wrappers. Old Blue was an absolute wreck that made Ray the butt of many jokes, but he didn't care. It didn't register on the list of what mattered to him. If he had to choose between his friends, family, and business or a clean car, the car was the loser. He had bigger things to concentrate on.

I know Ray had his share of heartbreak and loss. Like all of us, he trusted people who betrayed him. He bet on projects that didn't ultimately pan out. He dealt with setbacks and sorrows, as we all do. He never focused on the downturns, though, and he never let those losses keep him from trying again.

One incident summarizes his approach to life so well. A bunch of the kids and grandkids were hanging out at the restaurant my mother owned at the time. My son, Charlie, was a baby, so we were inside while the older grandkids were playing outside near a pond behind the restaurant. One of my older nephews, Justin, was about twelve. He was trying to catch a baby gator in the pond. He'd lure it with a fishing line, and then the line would break, and he'd start over again. Finally, he got that gator out of the pond and up onto the grass. The kids were shrieking with equal parts terror and excitement, and all the noise caught the attention of one of the adults. My sister Sherry came running in, shouting to Ray, "Justin's got that gator, and it's gonna eat one of those kids!" Cool as could be, Ray looked at her and said, "Well, he can't eat 'em all."

Calm in the face of chaos with an added sprinkle of wit, that was pure Ray. (By the way, the grandkids all survived.)

Watching Ray navigate life and business taught me so much. Love others well. Take calculated risks. Have fun in the process. Figure out what is important to you and forget the other stuff. Recognize that life has ups and downs, and after every down, an up will come, and vice versa. Know you can recover if you get dealt a bad hand. Be ready to give help, but don't be afraid to ask for help, too. Create a vision, and then let others share that vision with you. Have some laughs along the way.

Each time throughout my career that I took on a new role or moved to a new location, I felt like I was starting over from scratch. In these times, I tried not to hold on to my past accomplishments and instead focus on what was awaiting me. As a result, I was better able to navigate the situations in front of me because I was more fully present instead of having one foot in the past, longing for what was.

It's easy to look back at what we've left behind and wish for things to return to where they were. If we do so, though, we are taking the biggest risk of all: we're risking sacrificing what could be for what no longer exists.

Some days, I miss the life I had when Chuck and I were raising our children together, and our days and our hearts were full with our small family. There are occasions when I close my eyes and can almost hear the kids squabbling over the television in the den, sense Chuck's presence in the next room, smell dinner cooking on the stove after a long day of work and school. Those years were golden and times I will always, always cherish. But I cannot live there. If I do, I will sacrifice the new opportunities that lie in front of me at this stage in my life.

Yes, I miss those times, but I cannot even think of them as "a loss." The experiences I had, the love I was able to give and receive, and the memories I made are not gone. I have learned that I can build and risk again while still keeping all those moments in my heart. They live there, along with Chuck, Ray, my mother, my sister and brother, and the friends and other relatives who have passed. I know, without a doubt, I will meet them again.

In the meantime, I'm betting on the here and now. I'm moving forward without forgetting the past but also without trying to remain there. I have a book to write, a message to share, people to meet, and friends and family to love. There will be lots of ups and some downs along the way. I'll win, and I'll lose. Some of my plans may get derailed. Some may succeed while others fail. I'm ready for the ride. And if a baby gator comes along and threatens to go after some of my big ideas, that's okay. As Ray would say, he can't eat 'em all.

CHAPTER 11

Hold On

*If you can force your heart and nerve and sinew
To serve your turn long after they are gone,
And so hold on when there is nothing in you
Except the Will which says to them: 'Hold on!' ...*

Loving someone with terminal cancer is an impossible task on so many levels. The outcome in Chuck's case, we knew, was inevitable. Despite the grace-filled years of stability and even improvement, at some point, his condition would worsen. When he did start to decline, in some ways, it was worse than the initial diagnosis because we knew what we would be facing all too soon.

As Chuck's illness progressed to its final stages, it became more and more difficult, far beyond what I had anticipated, mainly because there were more and more problems and challenges to navigate. As the main breadwinner for our family, it was necessary for me to keep functioning so I could provide for our financial needs. As the one doing the active parenting for our son and daughter, I also had to be the one to provide for my children's emotional needs. As a partner, I needed to be a rock of stability for Chuck. I had to keep all the balls in the air at all times, and if I dropped any one of them, it could be a disaster.

At the point where Chuck went into hospice care, both Suanne and Charlie were living at home. We had trained nursing care for Chuck twenty hours a day from 8 a.m. to 6 p.m. and then again from 10 p.m. to 8 a.m. the next morning. During the four remaining hours in the evening, we'd have our family time, and I'd take over the main caretaking.

Day after day, we kept this schedule. I was drained, completely and utterly. The only time I seemed to get any sort of break was when I'd run out to pick up dinner from a local restaurant or do a quick errand. "Self-care" was sitting in my car for five minutes in the supermarket parking lot, trying not to feel too guilty about being away from home. It was surreal — wanting with every fiber in my being to hold on to Chuck as long as we could, for every second that God would allow us to have him, while also watching his physical and mental deterioration and wondering how much longer we could stand to see what this illness was doing to him.

I had so many conversations with both kids, urging them to embrace every day, even though it was breaking our hearts.

When I think back to how I was able to hold on, I recall what a minister friend of mine told us when Chuck was first hospitalized. I had reached out to this friend and told him what was going on, and he came to pray with us the morning Chuck was going in for his first biopsy. My friend told us to keep our eyes on the Lord and off the problem. That was the most profound statement under these circumstances, and it remained such a guiding principle when I felt like I absolutely couldn't handle any more.

The truth was, I couldn't handle any more. Chuck couldn't; the kids couldn't; Chuck's family couldn't. We were all overwhelmed with grief and were at the end of our limits.

We couldn't take it ... but God could.

That realization was one of the main ways I was able to show up, day after day, for everyone and everything that needed me when there was nothing left in me. When I accepted that I was powerless, I felt a little bit of relief because I was grounded in the belief that God was in control of the situation. I had to remind myself of that again and again.

Letting God be God didn't mean that I didn't do anything. I couldn't just bury my head and ignore everything around me. Instead, it was my job to keep my eyes on the Lord and trust in his ability to lead us all through this painful, horrible time. I let him direct my thinking, direct my actions, and direct my awareness. I couldn't heal Chuck, but I could make him more comfortable and provide the resources for his care and for our family. I could stay close to God, lean on him, pray a lot, and ask for guidance, strength, and emotional stability.

Chuck was not always the nicest person during the later stages of his illness. Anyone in a similar situation would be struggling to process the disease, the idea of mortality, and the loss of independence and function. When you add on the damage the tumor and subsequent operations did to his brain, it's completely understandable that his personality had been affected. Everyone had always described Chuck as just the nicest guy. Everyone loved him. But now, he could be difficult, testy, and impatient, and I had to bite my tongue many, many times. I reminded myself that this wasn't the real Chuck, and I worked to separate him from the effects of his illness. I could hold on to what I knew to be true about him and remember who he really was.

I would also ask myself if dealing with the ups and downs was worth it, and the answer was always yes. I knew I would rather have him in any capacity than not have him at all. Yes, it was a torment to see him in that state, but I knew he wasn't suffering. The thing about brain cancer is it's not painful the way other cancers can be. Chuck was on morphine for headaches, but it was not debilitating. So in my mind, it wasn't selfish to hold on to him for another day, another week, or another month if we could.

At some point, though, the time to let go comes. I learned this when my mother died. Her hospice nurse had told all of us that she needed permission to let go, and I sensed the time was coming for Chuck. I can't say I know where that point is for others, but it became clear to us that the end was very, very near. We were holding on, but it was time to let go and give him permission to do so, too.

I was able to share everything he needed to hear. I told him how much we all loved him. I told him he'd been a wonderful father. I told him he'd been a great husband. I told him that we would miss him and that I was so sorry that he had had to experience this illness. I told him he'd fought a good fight, and God was trying to bring him home. I told him we would be okay. And then

I told him he needed to give himself permission to let go and to be with the Lord.

And soon, he did.

It's impossible to explain how much of an impact losing a spouse, a father, a friend, a son, or a brother can have. It would have been so easy for me to let my heart die with him. But at that time, I knew I had to hold on in a different way. Now, I had to hold onto life. I had to fulfill the promise I made to Chuck that the kids and I would be okay after he was gone.

"Being okay" didn't mean we wouldn't feel the devastation of his absence. It didn't mean we didn't miss him every second of every day. For a very long time — months — I wasn't able to fully grieve. I threw myself into work, and when I traveled, it was easier because I wasn't in our house, surrounded by our things and our memories. Instead, I was in city after city, hotel room after hotel room. For a long time, I didn't even leave my room outside of my work meetings. I'd stay huddled in my bed, so numb from everything I'd been through that I couldn't even cry. I'd been in "hold on" mode and knew I needed to transition to "let go" mode. That shift was not easy. It took time. But one day, the dam burst, and the tears came.

What I learned is that grief has its own agenda. If you've had a loss in your life, people will have all sorts of suggestions and timelines for you. Some will tell you that it takes six months, or it takes a year, or that it's too soon to do this, or it's time for you to do this other thing. There is no timeline other than giving yourself the space and time you need to process and heal. In fact, the only wrong way to grieve is to try to rush through it.

Whether you've lost a loved one, a relationship, a job, or anything else you've loved, you have to let yourself feel the feelings. And if, like me, you were operating in "holding on" mode for a long time, you may not even know what you are feeling. That's okay. Be patient. Give yourself space. Don't rush.

A few months ago, I was on TikTok and came across a video of a man who had lost his wife several months prior. He was talking about dating again and mentioned that he wanted to find someone to grieve with him. I wanted to leave a comment that if he was still actively grieving and looking for a companion to grieve with him, maybe he shouldn't be dating! It isn't anyone else's job to process those emotions. That is his one and only job at this time, and he should take time to do it. Delaying or hiding the grieving process — or trying to outsource it to someone else — doesn't work.

Grieving is part of living. I think we try to cut this process short because it is not fun or comfortable. It is messy and unpredictable, and it requires us to feel things we'd rather hide away. When we give in to it, it can feel like the tears will never end. But they do. And even if they come again (and they probably will), they will stop.

On the other end of the spectrum are those who hold on to grief. It becomes the thing that defines them, and they are never able to move past it. While we don't want to resist our grief, we also don't want to live in it, making it our identity. It would be so easy to do that because we are hurting, and we don't want to risk living and then getting hurt again. But holding onto grief is a false sense of security. It won't keep you safe. It just keeps you stuck.

Eventually, on those business trips, I got tired of hiding out in my cocoon in the hotel room, just sitting with my thoughts. Eventually, I started to venture out, a step at a time. I would go to dinner or to a game or a show all by myself. I'd meet up with friends. And at a certain point, I even started extending my trip a few days to explore the city I was in. I began to create a new kind of life for myself. I began to feel okay again. I will never be the same, but I am okay, just as I promised Chuck.

When I feel the waves of grief rising up again and I wonder how I will make it through, I remind myself that I've done hard things before. I know how to do this. I just need to keep breathing, a day at a time or a minute at a time, if that's all I can do. I keep my eyes on God, not on the problem. And I hold on — to God and to life.

CHAPTER 12

Virtue

If you can talk with crowds and keep your virtue,
Or walk with Kings — nor lose the common touch ...

A few years ago, I was at a big annual conference when I ran into an old acquaintance. I knew she was supposed to be at a celebratory awards dinner, so I was surprised that she was in the hotel elevator instead. When I asked her why she wasn't at the dinner, she answered, "I'm not going to that. There are too many people I don't want to run into — and they certainly don't want to see me." I don't know if she's right about the other attendees, but I do know that it's sad that she can't even sit down at dinner with them.

Unfortunately, this occurrence isn't all that rare. I know many people from all walks of life who spend a lot of time and energy trying to avoid running into former coworkers, bosses, or direct reports — or ex-friends, neighbors, or significant others — because they ended things on a bad note. What a waste!

Here's an adage I learned pretty quickly: it's a small world out there. In other words, you never know when you're going to move to a new position and find yourself working alongside someone you knew from years before, often in entirely new roles with new responsibilities. Or your kids move to a new grade, and you suddenly find yourself on a committee with a parent you thought you'd left behind after the preschool years.

My former company has about 19,000 agents and 61,000 employees. It's not unusual, especially at the higher levels, to relocate across the country every few years. You might think that with so many people spread throughout the entire company, the chances of running into any one particular person once you've both moved on are pretty slim, but you'd be wrong! I've lost count of the times I've moved from one role in one state to an entirely different role in another state, only to find myself with familiar faces.

One time in particular was with Victor, my mentee, who was promoted to a field executive role to replace me as I moved to a new position. Then, a few years later, under a reorganization, we both ended up in the same department — where I was *his* direct report. The reverse has happened as well, where I eventually became the manager for someone who had been my manager in a previous position. Even though we'd had some differences of opinion when I reported to him, we'd always kept things cordial, and I was always respectful of his position. When we found ourselves with our roles reversed, I was able to greet him warmly and tell him truthfully that I was glad we were working together.

It's easy to let disagreements get the best of a relationship. It's understandable. When a relationship ends in our personal life, it's usually for a reason — your values were misaligned, your expectations were different, or you simply didn't mesh. Emotions can run high, and you can end the connection on less-than-positive terms. In work situations, you might be inclined to leave a piece of your mind as you leave the position but resist the temptation.

Isn't it better to never have to worry about running into someone you used to know? Even if you're moving companies and don't plan to ever run into these coworkers again, here's what I suggest: assume that one day you will indeed be working side-by-side with them, so keep the relationship cordial and do everything in your power to part on positive terms.

As my stepfather Ray used to say, "Be careful who you step on on the way up because you might meet them again on the way back down."

As wise as that statement is, I have found that it's even wiser to simply treat everyone you meet with respect and courtesy. If you can take the high road, even when you don't feel like it, you'll never worry about who you're sitting next to at the awards banquet.

For me, this sometimes takes effort. There have been times of fierce disagreement, times when I've questioned others' decisions, times when my ego got the best of me, and times when I couldn't wait to say goodbye. I'm only human, after all. But by keeping my mind on the end goal — the good of the organization — I was almost always able to move beyond my personal feelings and get to a place of respect.

On the other side of the spectrum are those whose treatment of others depends entirely on what they think the other can provide them. We all know people like this. They're overly polite and gracious to those further up the social ladder or the chain of command. Everyone they see as below them, though, is either ignored or treated poorly. It's always a surprise to them when someone they deemed "unworthy" ends up in a position of influence, but by then, it's typically too late to recover.

What amazes me is the rare person who seems to genuinely love everyone. It's like they see the people around them through love-colored glasses and don't let the little things like personality or title get in the way. Cate Ducato is one of these people.

Cate is the daughter of a sorority sister of mine, Carole. I knew the moment I met her that there was something different about her — and it was not because she has a genetic developmental disorder called Williams syndrome (WS). WS affects many bodily systems, including cognitive development.

Cate is different from most people because she is the embodiment of never "losing the common touch." She loves people right where they are and treats everyone the same, regardless of their income, education level, background, or looks. She has an uncanny ability to see through the externals and get to someone's heart, knowing intuitively if they are hurting and then loving them unreservedly.

Cate, who is twenty-four now, doesn't care if you're president of the company or the janitor responsible for emptying the trash. She doesn't distinguish between someone who can "do" something for her and someone who doesn't have a dollar to their name. Despite the challenges she faces, she is incredibly self-assured, confident, empathetic, and loving. In a word, she is a person of virtue.

She seems to see everyone she meets as a potential friend. You're a human, she's a human, and that's enough. And because of her pure love and openness, she manages to connect with people who aren't necessarily open in other relationships or who may typically hold themselves at a distance.

People with Williams syndrome are known for being kind, open, joyful, and loving. I'd venture that Cate is remarkable, even among others with the same condition. I give a lot of the credit for her confidence and joy to her parents, Carole and Carl, as well as to her two sisters, Caroline and Claire.

When you talk to Carole and Carl, they make it clear that Cate is not a burden and that the family never saw themselves as "chosen" by God to be entrusted with her care — in fact, it was the opposite. "It became really obvious that God didn't send Cate to be taken care of," says Carl. "Instead, God sent Cate to take care of Carole and me and the rest of the family. That's the thing that is always front and center for me, the difference she made for our family and truly anyone she has come in contact with, even as a little toddler."

From her earliest years, Cate seemed to be able to sense when someone was hurting, even when their pain was invisible to everyone else. "If we were in a group of people, she'd go right to the person who was hurting the worst, always. We never knew how — but she just knew," recalls Carl. One time Carole recalls specifically is when one of her nieces was struggling with some issues as a teenager.

Cate was in elementary school at the time and didn't know that her cousin was having problems, but apparently, she sensed it. "A group of kids were just sitting around talking, and she went up to my niece and said, 'You know, Jesus loves you, right?' It really touched my niece, and she still remembers it to this day."

God, say Carole and Carl, has given Cate the ability to see sadness in others in a unique way. Cate is touched by other people's emotions in a way that makes her want to share her joy with them. "He's given her the ability to see it and recognize it, and then he's given her the strength of character to be able to say something to try and help," Carole explains.

Having Cate in my life has made me ask myself if I also have that gift but have chosen not to use it. How often do I take the time to sense how others around me are feeling and ask what I can do to help? How often do I make assumptions about others based on their outward appearances, thinking either that they're so successful they couldn't possibly have anything less than a perfect life — or think that their challenging circumstances must be the result of their own poor choices or lack of willingness to work hard? How often do I stop myself from reaching out because I don't want to be rejected or I worry I might offend someone?

I guarantee that Cate never asks those questions. She doesn't talk herself out of opening her heart to others. To her, it's very simple. She sees someone hurting and reaches out to help. "She picks up on all the tiny little cues that most of us just, frankly, aren't in tune with or are just too busy to even notice," Carole says.

When I ask Carole what she's learned from Cate, she tears up. "Years ago, we were hanging out on the beach early one morning, walking and looking for seashells. I was trying to find just the pretty big, whole ones — you know, the special ones. Cate, who was probably in middle school, was running and picking up every piece of every shell and bringing them back to me, saying, 'Mom, look at how pretty! This one is beautiful!' and then she took another piece of a shell and said, 'Mom! This one is beautiful.' And I remember thinking, here I am looking for perfection, just the perfect seashell, and I have a daughter that many would think is flawed in a lot of ways. But she saw beauty in every single broken piece, and that's the way she is in life. She sees beauty in every broken person, in every broken situation. She finds the beauty, and that's what she focuses on."

Of course, I had to ask Cate what she thought people should know about her. "I love having Williams syndrome," she says immediately. "It's really awesome. And I want to tell people, if you have a child with Williams syndrome, I'm really happy to have it."

Talk about looking on the bright side and finding the beauty in everything. What could be more virtuous than that?

CHAPTER 13

Resilience and Emotional Stability

If neither foes nor loving friends can hurt you ...

So much of what Rudyard Kipling puts forth in his poem is about balance, and rightfully so. Balance is, after all, a marker of maturity: the ability to walk the line between being wise without acting too smart. Between triumph and disaster. Between walking with kings and losing the common touch. And in this line, the balance between opening up to others and their input without allowing it to steal your peace.

When I think back to the early years of my career, I knew I had intelligence, skill, and potential. What I did not have, though, was the trust and confidence in myself that can only be earned, not given. I needed to earn it the hard way, like everyone else — through years of practice and experience. Only by creating a foundation of stability could I then learn to weather the ups and downs of business and life. Without that hard-won stability, I was victim to the moods, input, and opinions of others.

This became very clear to me when my lack of confidence and my mindset almost derailed me.

It was the early 2000s, and I had been tapped to participate in our company's high potential developmental program, a stepping stone on the path to the corporate executive level. My colleagues and I were exposed to different leadership programs around the country, and this one in particular was one of the best developmental programs I'd ever experienced. I'd been exposed to the tactical — or more managerial — side of leadership, but this was the first time anyone had ever laid out the exact qualities of effective leaders based on hundreds of interviews with effective leaders.

The program was all day for five days in a row, from breakfast through dinner. It was intense but in a good way.

Then, one night, we were at a dinner session, and I just happened to be sitting at the table with the trainer. As was typical in those days, of the fifteen or so people in the program, at least a dozen of them were men. The conversation around the table that night included a lot of one-upmanship and a lot of intense debates. I didn't want to add to the conversation just to be saying something, so I stayed quiet, saying very little.

The trainer was also fairly quiet, taking it all in, and the whole meal just felt "off" to me. I finally did offer an opinion on something, and I sensed his body language shift.

When we returned to the main session, that "off" feeling continued, and the following presentation felt like it was directed right at me. "A single utter," the trainer said. "That's all it takes to derail your career." Maybe it was my imagination, and perhaps I was reading too much into it, but I thought he was aiming his remarks at me. It was like there was a spotlight on me in the room.

I began to get more and more uncomfortable as panic and an overwhelming anxiety started to bubble up in me. *A single utter?* I was thinking. *All it takes is saying one wrong thing at the wrong time, and then my career is over? Maybe I blew it at dinner — that's what he's talking about!* I simply was not at all certain I could live under that type of scrutiny and pressure and the constant stress of not making a mistake.

Up until that point in my career, I'd always been told that honest mistakes were part of development. I thought that as long as I came at things with honesty and integrity and understood the legal and compliance guidelines around my job, that would be enough. And now, someone was telling me that I could be demoted or even terminated for one verbal misstep. What had I gotten myself into?

I went back to my room that night a bit in shock, then woke up in the middle of the night in pure panic. *I can't do this*, I kept thinking. I had already been identified as "highpo," meaning I was a high producer and was someone with high potential. I had already committed to this development program. The company was investing in me with the understanding that if all went as planned, I'd be moved into an executive position. But was this right for me? I wasn't sure this was what I wanted anymore. Could

I put my fears aside to continue to move forward? Could I give what this path would require of me?

After all, the job was secondary to my family. What I loved most was being a wife and a mother. Yes, I loved my job, but did I want to live under that kind of pressure?

I continued to wrestle with these thoughts for the rest of the program. When I got back to my home office, I met with my sponsor, who was my boss's boss. When she asked me how the training had gone, I was honest. I told her about my misgivings and my lack of confidence. She listened and then said to me, "I'm not going to tell you you shouldn't feel that way because this next step is absolutely not for the faint of heart. You've got to be able to handle the pressure. You have to have self-assurance and confidence in yourself."

For weeks, I went back and forth with the idea of removing myself from the "highpo" list. After all, I had young children, and this was the same time when my mother was ill, so I had very rational excuses for saying, "No, thanks." But it wasn't sitting right with me.

I spent so much time talking to myself and evaluating myself as a person and a leader, trying to figure out what the next right step was. Until that time, my professional confidence was something I'd been working to develop. I knew I had some growth to do in that area, but I also believed I was capable of that growth. I knew I had what it took and wanted to see how far I could go. One side of me also said, "Yes, but that comes at a cost ... are you willing to pay it? Are you willing to watch every word you say and every move you make? Are you going to be willing to follow this long list of dos and don'ts to stay safe?"

I got to the point where I recalled something I'd heard the preacher of a small church say. He was telling a story about somebody who said a curse word and then said, "Oh, preacher, I'm sorry that slipped out." The preacher told him, "It wouldn't have come out if it wasn't in there."

I remember thinking about this in the context of me and the "single utter" that could destroy my career. I finally understood. *If it wasn't in there, it's not going to come out.* This wasn't about managing my *behavior.* This was about managing my *mindset* — my values and my belief system.

Why would I think that I would say something stupid or utter the wrong thing that could derail my career? Sure, I had made plenty of mistakes earlier when I was learning and growing, but I'd learned from them. That's part of the process for all leaders, but you mature past that stage. I knew who I was. I was thoughtful. I was smart. I had a good head on my shoulders. So why would I possibly think I'd suddenly say something career-ending? It wasn't in me.

Yes, I needed to be conscious of the situations I was in, and I'd always need to continue to build my emotional stability and my emotional management, just as every leader should. But the fear of derailing my career by some bombshell mistake was very unlikely. It wasn't a matter of watching what I said but, instead, watching who I was, and I was confident in that. I didn't have to act as anything other than who I was at the core, trusting that my authentic self would know what to do based on my values and beliefs.

That realization gave me so much freedom. The "single utter" was not something I needed to fear because I'd spent time and energy building my foundation.

What others thought of me — friends or foes — didn't matter, either. The only thing that did matter was that I could look at myself in the mirror and feel good about who I was.

As I moved to higher-level leadership, I started seeing more and more examples of people who are under extreme personal pressure and professional stress simply because they hadn't undertaken that fundamental shift of focusing on beliefs instead of behavior. Leadership and emotional stability aren't about what you say or do in any one meeting. They are about how you prepare yourself for meeting after meeting after meeting and how you show up in your true, authentic way.

Earlier in our lives, we are looking for clear, concrete guidelines — a playbook that tells us the step-by-step approach to success. We want a roadmap for how to behave in any given situation. We teach our children to say "please" and "thank you," "yes, ma'am," and "no, sir." We learn through repetition and rules. But as we mature, life becomes more complex. What works in one situation may not work in another. The universe gets much broader, and there are more choices. You can no longer rely on rules because you don't have a set of specific guidelines for each and every situation.

You also can't always rely on feedback from others. Some people will like what you do, and some won't. In a leadership position, it's rare that you make a decision that's unanimously approved by everyone. Instead, you have to rely on yourself. You have to trust your own judgment and your ability to adjust and pivot as things change. If you're looking for validation from external sources or you're trying to avoid criticism, you're going to be in trouble. You cannot lead by committee.

This isn't to say that good leaders don't seek counsel from others. They do. But they also know how to interpret that input. It's easy to let your emotions run away with you. We're influenced by so many things: what's happening in the current society, what our friends say, what our detractors say.

To me, emotional stability means being able to sort through the input, make decisions based on values, and deal with the consequences. It means you've learned to avoid the big swings to the highs and the lows. It's knowing that the bad's not as bad as it could be, the good may not be as good as you want it to be, and both are fleeting. You don't let the positive or the negative — the compliments or the criticisms — throw you off your game. When you do make a mistake or need to readjust, you might temporarily feel upset, but you get to choose how long you stay in that emotion. You can use self-talk to manage your emotions. Feel what you are feeling, but remind yourself that tomorrow, next week, next month, and next year, you won't feel as bad as you do right now.

I was counseling an agent who was dealing with a client who was somewhat of a bully, criticizing everything this agent did and constantly belittling everything from the service he received to the agent's intelligence. The agent asked me to help him strategize an upcoming conversation. "If he says this, what should I say? And if he says that, what should I say? What about this, this, or this?" the agent asked, full of anxiety. "Stop focusing on the details and focus on your desired outcome," I told him. "You'll make yourself crazy trying to prepare for every eventuality, so instead, just focus on who you want to be in that conversation." The agent relaxed. "I want to be polite, but I also want to draw a line." I could see he understood what I was trying to explain. It wasn't about the customer or who he was being. It was about the agent and who *he* wanted to be. This applies to our personal lives as well. Some people want to push our buttons and make every attempt to do so. You can't control their side of the conversation, but you can control yours.

That's emotional stability. That's maturity. When you keep that in mind, it doesn't matter what anyone else says or does. You're in control.

CHAPTER 14

Forgiveness and the Future Self

If all men count with you, but none too much ...

Nothing will refine your decision-making abilities more than being a working parent. It's a constant process of balancing competing priorities and figuring out whose needs are going to take the lead on which day. I did this dance for decades. Sometimes I got it right, and sometimes I didn't. It wasn't possible to do it all, and, more often than not, something had to give.

One day, when my son, Charlie, was about twelve or thirteen, we were in the car on our way to school, and he asked me, "Mom, why don't you have any friends?"

I kind of laughed and said, "I do have friends!" And then, I started naming the women I thought were my friends. "Janie is my friend. And so is Connie."

"No," he said. "Janie's your sister, and Connie works with you."

"Well, what about Jenny? I'm friends with her," I said.

"Jenny is Taylor's mom. And Taylor is Suanne's friend."

"She's still my friend," I insisted.

"What do you do with her? Do you play tennis or go shopping?" Charlie asked.

After I thought about it for a few minutes, I finally had to admit that according to Charlie's definition, I didn't have friends. In fact, while Chuck and I had four or five couples we socialized with, there wasn't really anyone outside my work or my family that I considered a friend. It just wasn't a priority at that point in my life. I was fulfilled by my work and my family, and I only had a certain amount of capacity. We had a lot of people who cared about us, and we considered them friends, but they were really acquaintances.

That day, Charlie even went as far as to say, "You don't get on the phone and talk to people like friends. You know, just sit on the phone and talk." And he was right. I didn't do that. I told myself I just didn't have the time. In actuality, it was a choice I was making without consciously making it.

At about the same time, Suanne was participating in competitive cheerleading, so she was always at the gym. Our nanny would drop her off at the gym, and then I'd pick her up on my way home from the office. I'd come into the gym in my professional attire — suit, heels — and sit there on my BlackBerry, reading emails and getting some work done.

I noticed the other moms weren't engaging with me. It didn't bother me because I was still in work mode. But Suanne said to me one day, "Mom, did you see me do that roundoff back handspring tuck?" I had to say no because I'd been answering emails. She thought about that and then said, "I want you to dress like the other moms at practice."

I was a bit taken aback and asked her why. She said, "All the other moms sit on the floor. They have jeans or shorts on, and you're sitting on the sofa because you're in heels and in your suit. I want you to be with the other moms."

I had never realized that the other parents sat in a very specific place where they could watch the girls practicing. I was friendly, but I wasn't intentionally engaging with them or watching my child. I was just doing my thing. So the next day, I packed some jeans, a T-shirt, and some tennis shoes, and I changed before leaving the office. Then I walked into the gym, said hello, and sat down in the group with everyone else. I put down my BlackBerry, watched my daughter, and became friendly with these women. Over time, those relationships grew to the point that we would travel to our competitions together, and we all got very close. All because I changed where I sat and what I wore when I went to pick my daughter up from practice.

It was amazing how this child, who at the time was probably only eight years old, saw how I dressed and was perceptive enough to recognize that she thought if I wore jeans and sat on the floor, then I could be friends with the other ladies. Even though Charlie might not consider these to be *my* friends, I did.

When Suanne brought my behavior to my attention, I could then shift my *intention*. I could look at my past behaviors, evaluate the results, and then make better decisions based on what I wanted the outcome to be. Because of the questions my kids had asked me, I realized I wanted to be more connected to the people in my life. I wanted my children to feel like I was paying attention to them when I was with them, not always on my phone or working. When I thought about what I wanted my outcome to be — what I wanted for my future self — I realized my actions didn't line up, and I could make a change.

I could also have compassion for myself. As the saying goes, when we know better, we do better. And doing better is a sign of growth. This is a lesson I'd learn again and again throughout my life.

One of the best — and hardest — things we did as a family when Chuck was entering the last phase of his illness was grief counseling. It may sound odd, and at first, I had some doubts about it, but one of the social workers on our hospice team asked us to consider having the chaplain come and start working with us. She saw how much we were struggling and thought having the opportunity to talk through our emotions and experiences would help.

Oftentimes, the patient themselves is struggling with their situation. Not only are they dealing with the everyday challenges of their decline, but they're also worried about the family they are going to leave behind. The family, of course, is grieving the impending loss of someone they love. By engaging together in the grief process, everyone would benefit by talking openly about what our concerns and fears were. It helped us talk about what was to come and how our lives were going to change, and it gave Chuck the opportunity to share his hopes and dreams for our futures.

This concept of "future self" was actually something I thought about a lot in the years after Chuck's diagnosis, and it's something I reminded Charlie and Suanne about repeatedly. What did we need to do today so that months or years from now, our future selves would look back and be proud of how we'd handled an unthinkable situation? How we acted in the present, I reminded myself and them, would either be a gift to or a burden of guilt and regret for our future selves.

You can take that thinking to a whole new level if you can consciously consider your future self. After all, tomorrow, you'll be looking back on today and asking, "How did I handle today? What do I wish I'd done differently? What can I change so tomorrow is better than today?"

In our family's case, we had already decided that we would give Chuck everything he needed to move through this time with as much comfort, security, and love as possible. Whatever it took, we would provide it. And it took a lot. We moved states; we moved houses; we drove hours on a regular basis back to Florida so he could continue his care at what we had decided was the best cancer facility for him. We hired nurses, and we set up the house so he could be in the middle of the family interactions, even as his mobility declined. I took it upon myself to learn as much as I could about his disease and its treatment so I could ensure he would always get the best possible care. Charlie and Suanne moved home so we could be together as a family. There were so many choices we made so we could support him mentally, physically, emotionally, and spiritually.

At the same time, though, we were each hurting, and we were all grieving differently. Suanne and Charlie were barely young adults at the time Chuck died, and much of their youth had revolved around their father. As much as I had tried to be present for them, the reality was that Chuck was the center point of our lives, and that took its toll. With so much of our time and energy focused on him, other things got pushed to the side.

At one point, the emotions in our household were running so high that one of our home care nurses, Juanita, called us together and called us out. She could see that the family dynamics were not healthy for any of us. We needed to have grace for ourselves and for each other, but we also needed to be clear about how we wanted to remember ourselves during this time. Our behaviors now would determine how we would feel in the future. Just like I'd made changes with the moms at the gym, we all needed to evaluate how we were handling this time to make sure it lined up with our desired outcomes. Would we look back with love and pride or with regret?

When you're in an incredibly challenging and emotionally charged situation, chances are, it will be a combination of both love and regret. We are human, after all. We can't always act as our best and highest selves. We get impatient; we get angry; we get hurt. And those emotions make their way into our behavior. Especially when someone is young, it's unrealistic to expect them to be able to set aside their own wants and needs to put someone else first, day after day.

Because we will make mistakes, we will need to have forgiveness for ourselves and for others. Speaking from a parent's point of view, there's a lot of stuff I have asked my kids to forgive me for over the years. I don't like all of the decisions I've made, and it can be very painful looking back. I can beat myself up, or I can forgive myself and move forward with greater understanding.

When I spoke recently with Charlie about this topic, he had so much wisdom to add. "There were so many times I did the opposite of what I wish I'd done," he said, recalling his father's illness. "I sort of ran away. I let the fear get to me, and it sent me down a path that was a little bit self-destructive." He said that looking back and realizing that there are things he wishes he'd handled differently can be painful.

The key he's found is to practice forgiveness. Forgiveness, particularly self-forgiveness, isn't something that happens all at once. It's something he returns to over and over, choosing what he wants for his life now and in the future. "I ask myself, 'How can I be a good friend? What kind of dad do I want to be to my kids? What kind of example do I want to set? What kind of man do I want to be? What are my goals?'" he said.

Forgiveness is like cleaning the slate and then writing something else on it, over and over, replacing guilt over the past with dreams and intentions for the future until they become reality. Charlie recalls something his father told him: happiness is having something to look forward to. Forgiveness also is a gift to your future self. It allows you to take the chains off and move forward into who and what you want to become.

CHAPTER 15

If

If you can fill the unforgiving minute
With sixty seconds' worth of distance run,
Yours is the Earth and everything that's in it,
And — which is more — you'll be a Man, my son!

As I looked out over the railing of the narrow balcony onto the busy streets of Paris below, I took a deep breath and tried to absorb all the emotions welling up in me. I was more than 4,000 miles from "home," but I wasn't feeling disoriented or lost. Instead, I felt more "me" than I had in a long time.

This hotel, this view, this trip — a month in Paris by myself, taking cooking classes at Le Cordon Bleu — had been a long time coming. It all represented a gift to myself after my retirement, but, in reality, it was so much more than that. It all also represented a convergence of events, people, decisions, and miracles throughout my whole life.

I knew the trip would be transformative, but when registering for my classes and figuring out logistics online from the comfort of my home in Atlanta, I couldn't even begin to imagine what it would be like to wake up every day in a foreign city where I knew no one and barely spoke the language. I looked at it as a grand adventure, an experience I might only have once in my life. Yes, I was a bit anxious, but more than that, I was filled with anticipation about what might occur.

I've loved cooking since I was old enough to stand at the kitchen counter alongside my mother. As the mother to seven kids, she was always busy, and it seemed like becoming her sous chef, even at the age of eight or nine, was the way I could get some time with her.

As I grew up, I worked in the food industry for many years, and my appreciation for cooking continued to grow. I never took "official" cooking classes. I just learned by observing and trying. But I have always wanted to learn more about the art of cooking, so when I retired, my daughter Suanne said, "Mom, you should go to Paris and take some culinary classes." At first, the idea sounded too ambitious, but over time, it began to take shape.

After a few delays due to COVID, I eventually found myself packing my bags. The stars had aligned. I'd spend a week in Munich with Suanne for a work trip, then my son Charlie and his girlfriend Shayne would meet us in Paris, where we'd all play tourist for several days. Then they'd leave, and I'd embark on my solo journey.

Even though I'd traveled by myself numerous times in my adult life, this felt different. I would have no colleagues I was meeting with, no office to show up at, and no agenda. It would be just me, myself, and I.

Even during our week together in Paris, staying at the Marriott near the Arc de Triomphe in the heart of the tourist district, I was waking up in the middle of the night in a panic, wondering whether I could be in this country after they left. But day by day, I got my bearings. In fact, as we walked around the city, Suanne insisted that I plan our excursions, doing everything from plotting our walking routes and leading the way to the Métro to requesting our rides on my phone. After a few missteps, I got in a groove.

One thing I hadn't decided yet, though, was where I was going to stay. While in the US, I'd spent hours looking at apartments online via VRBO and Airbnb. While there were some lovely options, many within a short distance of the cooking school, I couldn't choose. And while the Marriott had been perfect for our day trips around Paris, it was too far. So in the last few days of Suanne's visit, we went in search of the perfect location for me.

I started by eliminating the apartments. I knew if I had a kitchen and plenty of room to spread out, I'd be tempted to hole up, leaving only to attend classes. That wasn't what I wanted for this trip. I knew I needed to push myself to fully immerse myself in this new world. Choosing a hotel where I'd only have a room, rather than a fully-equipped home, would make me get out and about, exploring and interacting.

That decided, Suanne and I headed to the Marriott near Le Cordon Bleu.

The second I walked into the lobby, my stomach dropped. While it was a perfectly lovely hotel, I was transported back to my corporate days. I turned to Suanne and whispered, "This makes me feel like I have to check in, run up to my room, drop my bag, and then run to a conference room somewhere for a meeting. It makes me feel like I'm still working." As much as I loved that time in my life, I was in a different stage now, and I wanted to honor that.

We turned around and headed out the door. As we walked up the block, my eye was caught by the entryway to a building that was highlighted by a pink glow underneath a gorgeous wrought iron canopy. The placard read "M Social Hotel Paris," and I could not help but walk through the revolving door into the small foyer. The blend of old-world decor and modern lighting spoke to me immediately.

The clerk at the reception desk offered to have a bell-man show me a few rooms. The first room I saw was a very modest room overlooking an alleyway. Seeing our reaction, the bellman said, "There's another room I'd like to show you." We got back on the elevator, got off on the fourth floor, and walked down the hall to room 403. The second I walked in and saw the floor-to-ceiling windows, the balcony, and the lights to the left and right, I fell in love. I knew right then room 403 would be the room where I would spend the next several weeks — and I did. Room 403 became the safe place where I started each day and ended each evening. It was where I woke and greeted the morning with a "Hello, God," and thought about my intentions for the day ahead. It's where I packed my bag with my tablet and headed off for class or to a cafe, where I'd sit for hours and think and write. It was the place where I got dressed to take myself out to unexpected ad-ventures, like the haunted Paris tour, riverboat rides, and, of course, the many cabaret shows, like Moulin Rouge. It was my home.

The entire trip was such a gift — to and from my-self. I did whatever I wanted, met lovely people, explored, learned, and digested it all. Periods of instruction were broken up with hours of just sitting and reflecting. The weeks unfolded exactly as I'd hoped they would, a combi-nation of solitude and company, of activity and reflection, all the while marveling at both my past and all that is left to come. Strangely, separated from all that was familiar, I became more *me*.

I saw how every choice in my life had brought me to this place and how I still had so much more to live, do, and become. My book of life was full of chapters — some good, some bad, some comedies, some tragedies — but it all had led me to this moment, and I now could choose what I would write on the remaining pages.

Something as seemingly insignificant as the choice of where I'd stay became proof of how I desired to enter the next stage of my life as a different person than I'd been just five years before. My choice to intentionally interact and engage with the world around me made all the difference in my experience in Paris, and I didn't want to ever forget how being intentional about my days impacted me. When I told a dear friend about what I was experiencing, she put it so succinctly: "You looked in the mirror and said, 'I like her, and I want to see her again.'" I had seen a new version of me in Paris, and I wanted to bring her home with me.

Thankfully, that sense of wonder and excitement fol-lowed me home, packed in my suitcase with my souvenirs and clothes. Even now, months later, I work to recall the excitement I felt in Paris each morning, with a whole world to explore. I also see even more clearly how the stanzas of

Rudyard Kipling's poem weave together. The title itself — "If" — holds so much in just two letters.

The poem speaks to the options each and every one of us has in our lives.

Happiness and joy are not guaranteed.

Bravery and courage are not guaranteed.

Love and companionship are not guaranteed.

Riches and rewards are not guaranteed.

They are all conditional, based not upon what happens *to* us but rather upon what we make of what comes into our lives. It is the choices we make that bring us to where we are and what we have. And even in the times when we're dealt a rotten hand, or we end up somewhere we'd rather not be as the result of our own poor choices, we can choose what the next chapter of our life will be. This fact became so clear to me in Paris as I gave myself the space and time to evaluate, think, and dream.

Here's one thing I want to emphasize: you do not have to travel halfway across the world to reflect on your life and make different decisions about it. You can give yourself that same space and time to choose wherever you are.

Whether you're twenty-nine, fifty-nine, or ninety-nine, you can put forth the effort to be the best version of yourself each and every day. You don't have to fly to Paris and go to Le Cordon Bleu to find a new version of you. You can just be more intentional about how you want to show up at every moment of the day, whatever that day brings.

You can rise to the challenge Kipling has put in front of you — to be brave, patient, joyful, forgiving, virtuous, honorable, and more. And if you don't like what you did yesterday or last week or last year, you can do what my son Charlie recommended so wisely as he spoke about forgiveness. You can recognize how you have fallen short of your intentions, resolve to do better, let it go, and move on. Tomorrow will present another page to fill. "Yours is the Earth," as Kipling put it because you can choose and choose again.

Yes, some of your pages have been partially filled in with obligations and commitments. You can't always control what gets written. Some of your chapters are a lot more packed with work, kids, family, and other responsibilities, some you've chosen and some were chosen for you. Other chapters — like the one I'm writing now — have more room. No matter what, I believe there's always blank space in the margins that you get to fill in.

That is the beauty of "If" — both the poem and the word. It represents possibility and power. It offers freedom rather than dictating an outcome. Being willing to accept the responsibility that comes with freedom is much of what being an adult is all about. And knowing that you can always, always bounce back from any challenge or hardship means you've become a stainless steel butterfly.

You've learned to weather the storm.

You've learned to fly.

Acknowledgments

To my children, Charlie and Suanne. Thank you for your encouragement as I made the journey of writing this book. An extra thank you to Suanne, who said, "You should write a book, Mom," as I expressed my restlessness in retirement.

To Charles and Barbara Pinkard and my sister-in-law Susan. You have loved me and made me a part of your family from the day Chuck brought me home to meet you. You are more precious to me than you can ever know.

To Andy Andrews, *New York Times* bestselling author and my favorite author. Thank you for encouraging me to write this book. Being my first (and possibly only) book, your encouragement helped build my confidence to take the first step.

To Debra Boblitt, author of *Bold Mission: Courageously Pursue Your Calling.* Thank you for being my business and life coach throughout this process and for being my friend since 1993. Thank you to Nicole Gebhardt and the entire team at Niche Pressworks for all of your guidance and support.

To Lain Ehmann. Thank you for spending months working with me to make this book a reality.

To everyone who allowed me to tell their story as wonderful examples of the life principles I wanted to share and to those who contributed their thoughts and experiences: Angela Martin; Bill Roundtree; Carl, Carole, and Cate Ducato; Troy Wolkow; Ouida Brown-Lyon; Juanita; Jim; Joe; Victor, John Bowman, and Debra Helms. Thank you for trusting me to share you with my readers.

To Ray Dempsey, who gave me the poem "If" at such an important time in my life. Thank you for all you did for me and everyone in our family while you were here on earth. There would be no *Stainless Steel Butterfly* book without you.

To my incredible mother, who was the perfect example of a stainless steel butterfly. We all miss you! To my siblings Roberta, Janie, Sherry, Edward, Frank, and Michael — thank you for all my childhood memories and all the new memories we are making as adults.

To Chuck. Thank you for being a wonderful father and loving husband and showing us all how to fight for life during the most difficult times. We miss you but know you are always with us.

Most of all, thank you to God, who tugged at my heart until I took this step in obedience to him. I have no idea how this book might impact someone else's life, but you do. So, as I release it into the world, I trust you to place it in the right hands for your honor and glory!

About the Author

Susie Pinkard spent thirty-two years with a Fortune 50 insurance and financial services company. She started by owning her own business and then transitioned to the corporate division, where she held numerous executive positions. She served as agency vice president overseeing the development of rising executives. She is on the Jacksonville State University Foundation Board and was named JSU Alumna of the Year for 2023.

She and her late husband, Chuck, are the parents of two adult children, Charlie and Suanne.

Susie loves anything associated with the beach, water, and boats. She adores cooking, loves to learn, and is committed to filling the days of her life with friends, family, food, and her deep faith. Recently, she has found great joy reconnecting with people from her past who have influenced or touched her in some way.

Currently, Susie splits her time between Georgia and Orange Beach, Alabama.

To connect with Susie about speaking opportunities or other questions, please visit SusiePinkard.com.

Made in the USA
Columbia, SC
13 June 2024

a0015bdb-5a97-48ba-b73e-6ef8c5f7013dR01